CHILD POVERTY
IN IRELAND

Brian Nolan

Oak Tree Press

Dublin

in association with
Combat Poverty Agency

Oak Tree Press
Merrion Building
Lower Merrion Street
Dublin 2, Ireland
www.oaktreepress.com

A catalogue record of this book is
available from the British Library.

ISBN 1 86076 183-6

This study forms part of the Combat Poverty Agency's Research Series,
in which it is No. 30. The views expressed in this report are the authors'
own and not necessarily those of the Combat Poverty Agency.

Printed in the Republic of Ireland
by Colour Books Ltd.

Contents

Author's Acknowledgements

This study draws on the 1994 and 1997 waves of the Living in Ireland Survey, the Irish element of the European Community Household Panel. James Williams and Dorothy Watson of the ESRI's Survey Unit were responsible for the survey design, data collection and database creation for 1997, while the 1994 design, data collection and database creation were the responsibility of Brendan Whelan and James Williams. Helpful comments and suggestions on the study were received from the Combat Poverty Agency. Chapter 6 draws on work prepared as part of a UNICEF project on the dynamics of child poverty in industrialised countries, and benefited from helpful comments and advice from Bruce Bradbury, Markus Janti, Stephen Jenkins, John Micklewright and participants in a workshop at ICDC Florence in October 1998.

Foreword: Ending Child Poverty

WHY A FOCUS ON CHILD POVERTY?

Child poverty has long been a specific concern of the Combat Poverty Agency, as the statutory centre of expertise on the elimination and prevention of poverty. The Agency has produced various research and policy reports on this issue.[1] It has also supported innovative programmes which address aspects of child poverty, notably educational disadvantage and social exclusion in the border regions arising from the Northern Troubles.[2] Current Agency initiatives include identifying indi-

---

[1] Nolan, B. and Farrell, B. (1990), *Child Poverty in Ireland*, Dublin: Combat Poverty Agency; Millar, J. *et al*, (1992), *Lone Parents, Poverty and Public Policy*, Dublin: Combat Poverty Agency; O'Neill, C. (1992), *Telling It Like It Is*, Dublin: Combat Poverty Agency; B. Nolan (1993), *Reforming Child Income Support*, Dublin: Combat Poverty Agency; Carney, C. *et al* (1994), *The Cost of a Child*, Dublin: Combat Poverty Agency; Kellaghan, T. *et al* (1995), *Educational Disadvantage in Ireland*, Dublin: Department of Education and Combat Poverty Agency; Combat Poverty Agency (1998), *Investing in Children*, Submission on the 1999 Budget; Combat Poverty Agency (2000), *A Better Future for Children: Eliminating Poverty, Promoting Equality*, Submission on the National Children's Strategy.

[2] The Educational Disadvantage Demonstration Programme (1996-2000) supports four local networks tackling educational disadvantage using an integrated approach. The impact of and lessons from the programme are currently being assessed. The Agency co-administers elements of the EU Peace and Reconciliation programme in the southern border region. This role is set to continue under the successor programme, Peace II.

cators and targets for child welfare, developing new initiatives and policies to tackle child poverty and heightening public awareness of child poverty, including the *Open Your Eyes to Child Poverty Initiative*, in conjunction with six other organisations.[3]

The Agency has prioritised child poverty for the following reasons:

- Poverty gravely diminishes the living standards of affected children. Poor children not alone have fewer material goods and enjoy lower quality services than their better-off counterparts, but are less likely to participate in conventional child activities. Through an accident of birth, poor children are, in effect, excluded from society.

- Child poverty has many indirect effects on children's welfare, e.g. inferior housing conditions, increased risk of child abuse[4] and other social problems. Poor children are less likely to do well in school and are in poorer health. Child poverty can also worsen the situation of children experiencing discrimination, such as Travellers or those with disabilities.

- Child poverty is not just a transitory phase associated with childhood, but often has a legacy that persists in later life, regardless of children's talents or efforts. Adults who had poor childhoods have low educational attainment, restricted job prospects, lower incomes and a shorter life expectancy. Child poverty is thus at the root of an inter-generational cycle of poverty.

- From an economic perspective, child poverty represents a collective waste of human capital. This has a direct eco-

---

[3] These are Barnardos, Children's Rights Alliance, Focus Ireland, National Youth Council, Pavee Point and Society of St Vincent de Paul.

[4] Buckley, H. (1999), "Child Protection", in *Child Poverty: Issues and Solutions*, EAPN Ireland.

nomic cost in terms of loss of economic productivity and additional expenditure on compensatory measures. These costs are exacerbated in a context of labour market shortages and an ageing population.

The National Anti-Poverty Strategy, the government policy statement on poverty, has the following view of the significance of child poverty:

> (L)ack of an adequate income is only one aspect of child poverty. Poor children have been shown to do less well educationally, are more likely to suffer ill health, are vulnerable to homelessness and delinquent behaviour and fewer opportunities in life. Child poverty can seriously damage the life chances of many children, leading to a cycle of deprivation which repeats itself from generation to generation. [5]

Child poverty has also emerged as an issue at the international level, where there is a recognition of the special onus on society to protect children who, through no fault of their own, experience a deprived childhood. This obligation is formally recognised in the UN Convention on the Rights of the Child, to which Ireland is a signatory. The convention includes a commitment to an adequate standard of living as a basic right of all children and obliges governments to intervene where child poverty occurs. The particular challenge this poses for Ireland is highlighted in a recent national review by the UN Committee on the Rights of the Child.[6] It noted that child poverty in Ireland was undermining the fundamental rights of children, including their access to education, housing and health services. The committee called for immediate steps to tackle child poverty and to

---

[5] Ireland (1997), *Sharing in Progress. National Anti-Poverty Strategy*, Dublin: Stationery Office, p. 47.

[6] UN Committee on the Rights of the Child (1998), *Concluding Observations on the Report Submitted by Ireland Under Article 44 of the Convention.*

make all possible efforts to ensure that all families have adequate resources and facilities.

Meanwhile, the particular challenge of child poverty for rich industrialised nations such as Ireland has been highlighted by UNICEF. It notes that the combination of economic growth and rising living standards has not eliminated child poverty, as had been expected. UNICEF's recent report reveals that one in six of the world's richest children is poor. However, national child poverty rates vary considerably, reflecting economic circumstances and policy responses. Ireland is identified as among those countries with the highest rates of child poverty in the 23 OECD member states, whether using relative or absolute measures. UNICEF poses the following challenge for countries such as Ireland with high rates of child poverty:

> The persistence of child poverty in rich countries undermines both equality of opportunity and commonality of values. It therefore confronts the industrialised world with a test both of its ideals and of its capacity to resolve many of its most intractable social problems.[7]

This research report represents a contribution to the growing awareness and concern about child poverty. It is particularly timely for three reasons. First, it provides a backdrop to the preparation of the National Children's Strategy, the government initiative to advance the welfare of children in accordance with the UN Convention on the Rights of the Child.[8] Second, it gives an assessment of the impact of economic growth and government policy on child poverty rates during the 1990s, especially in the context of the National Anti-Poverty Strategy. Third, it indicates possible benchmark figures for child poverty reduction

---

[7] UNICEF (2000) *Innocenti Report Card* No 1; Florence: UNICEF.

[8] The findings of the research are incorporated into the Agency's submission on the strategy.

targets under an updated National Anti-Poverty Strategy, as proposed by the Minister for Social, Community and Family Affairs and the *Programme for Prosperity and Fairness*.

RESEARCH FINDINGS ON CHILD POVERTY

The research in this report provides baseline and longitudinal information on child poverty in Ireland, drawing primarily on the Living in Ireland Survey, a unique data source on the evolving incomes of a representative sample of households between 1994 and 1997. The data also facilitates comparison of the Irish situation with that in other European countries, through the European Community Household Panel Survey. The various research methodologies employed in the study give a comprehensive account of the nature and extent of child poverty at a household level. For comparative purposes, the definition of a child in the study is under 14 years old, but similar poverty trends are reported when older age cut-offs are applied (i.e. under 16 and 18 years).

The main findings in regard to the numbers experiencing child poverty in 1997 are:

- A quarter of children live in households below half average income, with almost two in five children below the 60 per cent relative income poverty line and 13 per cent below the 4 per cent line.[9] In absolute terms, there are between 130,000 and 370,000 children under the age of 18 years living in varying degrees of relative income poverty.

- Children are up to 1.25 times more likely to be in income poverty than adults. Irish children have the highest rate of

---

[9] The monetary value of the various poverty lines in 1997 were, for a two-adult, two-child household, the average weekly equivalent of £145.66 (40 per cent), £182.07 (50 per cent) and £218.49 (60 per cent). The average weekly household equivalent income per child was £21, £26 and £31 respectively.

income poverty in the EU, one-and-a-half times more than the average and similar only to Portugal and the UK (1994 data). Underlying this ranking is the high proportion of out-of-work families in Ireland.

• Seventeen per cent — 170,000 — of children are in consistent poverty, as measured by a combination of income poverty and non-monetary deprivation indicators. Also, children are twice as likely to experience consistent poverty as are adults.

The report highlights the following trends in child poverty over time:

• Child poverty has fallen in recent times, thereby reversing a long-term deterioration in the relative situation of children observed since the early 1970s. The improvement is greatest when the consistent poverty measure is used (down a third) or if 1987 poverty lines indexed by inflation are applied to 1997 (down a half). The gap in poverty risk between children and adults has also narrowed.

• About 10 per cent of children were below relative income poverty lines in both 1994 and 1995. However, those below the lowest income lines were most likely to show a considerable improvement in their position from one year to the next.

The study's examination of the family circumstances of poor children reveals that:

• Children in out-of-work families are at greatest risk of poverty (i.e. where a parent is unemployed, ill or disabled or engaged in home duties). Such families account for two-thirds of all poor children. This pattern is accentuated for children in consistent poverty, with over half in unemployed families alone. Though having a low poverty risk, working families still account for 30 per cent of poor children.

- Children in lone-parent and very large families are more likely to be poor. However, poor children are to be found in a variety of family sizes: two-fifths are in families with two adults and three plus children; a third are in families with older and younger children, 18 per cent are in smaller two-adult families and a tenth are in lone-parent households. Poor families are only slightly bigger than non-poor.

From the above findings, it is apparent that Ireland has a severe problem of child poverty. Child poverty affects between a sixth and a quarter of Irish children, depending on the measure, which, in absolute terms, amounts to up to a quarter of a million children under the age of 18 years. The vulnerability of children can also be gauged by their position compared either to adults or to their European peers. The concentration of poor children in families out-of-work and the high poverty risks for children in one-parent and larger families is also of concern. While the minority of children experience persistent poverty, many others are in poverty on an intermittent basis.

There is, however, some good news in the study, notably the improvement in the relative position of children compared to the 1980s and early 1990s and a narrowing differential between children and adults. The main driver here has been the fall in unemployment arising from economic growth. It is likely that the improvement in children's fortunes has arisen since 1997, as unemployment continued to decline. However, this trend is unlikely to affect significantly our ranking in terms of EU child poverty rates. This is because of the unequal distribution of work among families, with Ireland having a high percentage of families with no working adult. Thus, falling unemployment can go hand-in-hand with a growing polarity between work-rich and work-poor households. Complacency about the capacity of falling unemployment to automatically provide the solution to child poverty is therefore misguided.

Children in poverty have benefited from rising living standards in recent years, especially using absolute and consistent measures of poverty. However, these gains have been diluted by the failure to link increases in state child income support either to wage rises or general welfare increases. This is despite the record increase in child benefit in Budget 2000, which has to be set in the context of the total tax/welfare allocation of £1.6 billion. As a result, households on higher incomes have seen their living standards increase four times as much as low-income households, while non-child households will have gained over families. All this means that the relative position of welfare-dependant families will not have improved since 1997.

POLICY ISSUES

The overall conclusion of this study is that falling unemployment and rising personal incomes are not on their own sufficient to end child poverty. The challenge for government is proactively to redistribute resources in favour of children on the lowest incomes. A starting point for this is to have a much stronger focus on children in policy statements. There is an acknowledged lacuna in public policy when it comes to children. For too long, children's welfare has been treated as the primary responsibility of families. Reflecting the approach to the needs of children contained in the UN Convention on the Rights of the Child, future policy should be premised on an explicit acknowledgement of the rights of children to state-guaranteed minimum standards of living and other social entitlements. In addition, there is a need for a better integration of economic and social policies, so that the needs of children and families are reflected in economic policies. It is a mistake to separate jobs, tax and housing issues from consideration of how these impact on the quality of life for families and children.

Arising from these preliminary comments, a logical first step would be to prioritise child poverty in government policy, especially the National Anti-Poverty Strategy and the National Children's Strategy, but also the annual Budget statement. This would have as a core element the promotion of a child poverty reduction target. Such a target should be conceived of in terms of three separate components, as part of an overall strategy of abolishing all forms of child poverty in 20 years.[10]

- At a minimum, ensure that the incomes of poor children grow ahead of inflation and ideally in line with wages, in order to ensure an equitable share of the growing wealth of the economy.

- Abolish consistent child poverty (income poverty and deprivation) over ten years from 1997 (the same time period as the National Anti-Poverty Strategy).

- Reduce the proportion of children in income poverty by half in ten years and fully in twenty, with a faster fall in the number of very poor children.

These targets should be revised regularly to take account of rising living standards and trends in child poverty in the intervening years. The target of a 50 per cent reduction in child income poverty is in line with that recently proposed by the EU Commission at the Lisbon Heads of Government summit. Moreover, eliminating child poverty in 20 years corresponds to the target adopted by the UK government, which has a similar level of child poverty. The Agency proposes that the above targets are adopted both in a revised NAPS and in the forthcoming National Children's Strategy. In addition to monetary targets,

---

[10] For a discussion on the challenge of setting poverty targets in a growing economy, see Nolan, B. (2000) 'Targeting Poverty in the National Anti-Poverty Strategy", paper for combat Poverty Agency conference *Planning for a More Inclusive Society: the National Anti-Poverty Strategy*, May, 2000.

there should be targets for improvements in child welfare in terms of children's education, health, housing and special needs.

Having set child poverty targets, what actions are required to achieve these? The policy lesson from recent experience is that relying on the labour market to reduce child poverty is an inadequate response. In the Agency's view, a more proactive approach to child poverty is required, centred on three sets of actions: child income support, access to jobs and opportunities for social and educational development.

Child Income Support

Our current mixed system of child income support is the outcome of incremental policy changes over a period of time. This is not to criticise the recent shift in the provision of child income support from welfare schemes to universal support, but to note that it has not been sufficient in scale to tackle child poverty. Given the link between poor children and unemployed families, it is essential that work-neutral child support remains the policy strategy. However, to make major inroads on child poverty, the resources devoted to child support must be increased, whatever the policy guise, with the priority being those on low-incomes. In this context, key considerations are targeting children at high risk of poverty, improving the overall position of families, equal treatment of different types of families and integrating the diverse policy instruments used to support children. It is also important to realise that children in poverty are a fluid group. Hence, concentrating resources exclusively on those in greatest and persistent need may miss children whose exposure to poverty is short-term or linked to life-cycle events.

The Agency proposes the following package of reform:

- A minimum child income payment of £30-£40 per week, depending on the age of the child, should be provided for children in welfare-dependant families. It would be primarily delivered through a greatly enhanced child benefit (see below), with a means-tested supplement to ensure a minimally adequate amount. (This proposed income range is based on previous Agency research[11] and a revised estimation should be considered by the working group on the adequacy of welfare payments, to be set up under the *Programme for Prosperity and Fairness*). Additional support with the costs of education for low-income families should also be provided, both in cash and kind, to encourage school participation.

- Increase child benefit to £25 per week, as representing the state's share of two-thirds of the costs of a child. This would replace all other forms of child income support (e.g. FIS, CDAs), with the exception of a means-tested supplement for families on welfare, of £5–£15. Child benefit represents the fairest, most efficient and cost-effective way of supporting the costs of children. In particular, it avoids problems related to work incentives and family formation. It is also a child-targeted expenditure since it is both a ring-fenced child payment and is paid to the primary carer of children, the mother. Also, the main beneficiaries of child benefit are poor families, while it also promotes horizontal equity for all families. Finally, this would build on the commitment in the *Programme for Prosperity and Fairness* to increase the higher rate of child benefit to £100 per month (£23 per week).

- Child income support which relates to the care of children, including those with disabilities, should also be enhanced. State support for childcare is currently under review in the context of the *Programme for Prosperity and Fairness*. Given the evidence on child poverty, the high poverty risk for households not in work and with the need to enhance employment opportunities for unemployed/low-paid mothers,

---

[11] Carney, C. *et al* (1994), *op cit.*

provision in this regard should not favour taxpaying families or only those working outside the home. A universal child-care supplement for families is recommended as the best way forward, linked to child benefit. The Agency has previously identified the possibility of funding a monthly childcare supplement for all children of £32.50 by restricting the transferability of tax bands. A further source would be the home carers allowance, which could fund a cash benefit for all families of £5 per week. Meanwhile, the provision of income support for families with children with disabilities warrants further investigation.

We have estimated that the net cost of this reform of child income support would be in the region of £500 million per annum, phased in over three years (this figure does not take account of the government commitment in the *Programme for Prosperity and Fairness* to raise the higher rate of child benefit to £23 per week). This expenditure is clearly feasible given the surplus in the public finances and the indicative allocation of £1.5 billion on social inclusion measures in the *Programme for Prosperity and Fairness*. The cost can also be seen as incorporating an indirect tax reduction for better off families.

Access to Jobs

Better child income support should go hand in hand with measures to maximise employment opportunities for families, especially those with no one at work (hence, the emphasis on universal child benefit). Fiscal strategy should assist non-earning parents to access employment, to maximise overall hours at work and to meet childcare responsibilities, both at an individual and household basis. The earnings disregard for lone parents under the One Parent Family Benefit has proved quite effective in this regard. Extending these reforms to other low-income families should now be considered through changes in unemployment assistance and family income supplement.

Other measures such as an efficient system of public transport, accessible and affordable childcare services and retention of child-oriented benefits (e.g. medical card) are also proposed. It also suggested that labour market programmes better reflect the family circumstances of unemployed parents, both mothers and fathers.

Opportunities for Social and Educational Development

It is also important to address the lack of opportunities for poor children to better their situation, perpetuating childhood disadvantage into later life. The goal here is to maximise the social and educational development of poor children. Education is crucial in this regard, as are health and housing and family support services. Unfortunately, our current education system is far from achieving equality of opportunity. Early childhood education, in-school compensatory measures, retention programmes for older children and access programmes for third-level are required to address the structural imbalance in education. Other interventions which enhance the nutritional and health status of poor children, improve the physical and social environment in which children are brought up, provide sports and recreational facilities, assist children at risk of inappropriate behaviours (drugs, vandalism, crime) and tackle discriminatory practices which affect minority children such as Travellers, migrants, those with disabilities, are also proposed. (Details on proposed actions are contained in the Agency's submission on the National Children's Strategy.)

The role of parents in providing care for and nurturing their children has been largely neglected. The provision of services to families to support their caring role is only a recently emerging aspect of child welfare policy in this country. Otherwise, the main policy focus is on intervention in families where children are at risk of abuse. As such, family support policy has been more reactive than preventative in its focus. An important departure in this regard is the report of the Commission on the Family, which contains a range of proposals outlining how the role of families in caring for children can be strengthened. The Commission paid particular attention to the position of poor families raising children in difficult economic and social conditions, including those with one parent.12 The main instrument in this new approach to families under pressure is the growing network of family resource centres and related programmes under the auspices of the Department of Social, Community and Family Affairs. The health boards are also developing their role in supporting families, through initiatives such as the community mothers' programme and, more recently, the Springboard pilot initiative. Again, these supportive policies for families should be expanded. There is a clear need for better linkages between the various arms of the state in supporting families at the local level. Also, the contribution of community and voluntary organisations should be recognised, along with that of parents themselves.

There is a growing number of poor children who require special care and protection due to exposure to drugs, crime, prostitution, homelessness, begging, exploitative labour, displacement, physical/sexual abuse and political/military conflict. Existing provision of services for vulnerable children, while expanding, requires additional resources and better co-ordination. In addition, general services directed at social problems should incorporate an explicit focus on children and give equal consideration to their specific needs, especially where they may differ from and even be in conflict with the needs of adults.

ISSUES FOR RESEARCH

The study highlights research questions which warrant further data-gathering and analysis. In order to achieve a better under-

---

[12] Commission on the Family (1998), *Strengthening Families for Life*, Dublin: Stationery Office.

standing of child poverty, we require the development and application of a set of child-specific deprivation indicators. Such indicators are important on two accounts. First, to understand better the impact of poverty on children reflecting their exclusion from, enjoyment of, and participation in everyday activities. This is crucial in order to explore fully the non-monetary effect of child poverty, including its impact on the social development of children. Second, such indicators can better capture children who experience deprivation due to the unequal sharing or prioritisation of resources in families, including non-poor households. Already, the 1999 Living in Ireland Survey has includes some questions in relation to child-specific indicators of deprivation. A more comprehensive list of items, informed by qualitative research, might include the following:

- A birthday party with friends and relations
- Participation in after-school classes (drama, swimming, music)
- Involvement in organised sports or a club (scouts etc)
- An occasional family outing to the zoo, cinema or similar special event
- A breakfast with cereal and a hot dinner
- Fruit or vegetables four times a day
- Regular pocket money
- New toys on birthdays, Christmas or other special occasions
- School-related items (books, clothing, footwear, lunches, outings)
- Separate-sex bedrooms for older children (10+)
- Attendance at a doctor when a child is ill
- Special needs equipment, e.g. for a child with a disability
- A safe area in which to play with friends.

In addition to the above, it would also be useful to analyse the risk of child poverty for various age groups and to further explore the longitudinal aspects of child poverty.

We need to complement the quantitative approach of the Living in Ireland Survey, including the additional information mentioned above, with qualitative insights into the experiences of poor children. It is surprising how little has been documented about the experiences of children in poor families. Most research operates at the level of the family and seldom investigates the distinctive experience of poor children. For example, it would be helpful to know how poverty impacts on children's everyday lives, what their experiences of social services are and how they manage and react to circumstances shaped by poverty and deprivation. In addition, we are badly informed about the significance of children in poor families, especially in terms of allocation of household resources, development of parental skills access to employment, formation of relationships and interaction with neighbours, schools, etc. To remedy this research deficit, the Agency has recently initiated a qualitative study of low-income families in conjunction with the Department of Sociology and Social Policy at Queen's University Belfast. This study has as a particular theme the production of a child-centred account of life in poor families. It is expected that the results of the study will be available late next year.

Furthermore, child poverty is but one indicator of the welfare of child. Based on the UN Convention on the Rights of the Child, it is possible to identify four categories of child welfare: (a) material well-being; (b) health and survival; (c) education and personal development; and (d) participation and protection. The Agency has already undertaken some work, applying these categories of child welfare in the Irish context, both in terms of possible indicators and data collection. We have drawn on international studies, including a recent report by UNICEF on child welfare in Europe.[13] A possible list of indicators might be as follows:

Category I: Material Well-being

- Child poverty (income and deprivation)
- Unemployment among families
- Families in receipt of social welfare, in particular SWA
- Children's participation in the labour force
- Families in need of housing.

Category II: Health and Survival

- Mortality rate for children under 5
- Child suicide
- Child pedestrian/bicycle deaths
- Birth rate for teenagers
- Children using alcohol or drugs
- Children on hospital waiting lists.

Category III: Education

- Attendance at pre-school
- Child literacy
- Participation in education at age 15 years
- Non-attendance at school (including children excluded from school)
- Children with disabilities attending mainstream schools.

---

[13] Micklewright, J. and Stewart, K. (1999), *Is Child Welfare Converging in the European Union?* Innocenti Occasional Papers, Economic and Social Policy Series no 69, Florence: UNICEF Child Development Centre.

Category IV: Participation and Quality of Life

- Access to local recreational facilities
- Involvement in after-school activities (clubs etc.)
- Ability to influence decisions
- Children in care
- Children involved with the law
- Children out of home.

Data for the above indicators should largely be available or collectable by public agencies. Quality-of-life data and behavioural information may require specific research instruments. It is therefore proposed that the National Children's Strategy should institute a regular monitoring report on the welfare of children, following consultation on appropriate indicators and data requirements. In the meantime, the Agency will continue its work in this regard in order to inform future developments. It is also recommended that the government commission a national study of the quality of life of children, which could be conducted on a longitudinal basis. This would follow a cohort of children from birth onwards, giving a rounded account of their development over the period of their childhood. There is also a need for other, more specific, research on aspects of children's lives. This would require the establishment of a children's research fund, along the line of the family research fund.

In conclusion, we have the financial capacity now to eliminate child poverty, if the social commitment and political will also exist. Failure to tackle child poverty now would not be justifiable in economic or social terms.

Combat Poverty Agency
July 2000

Chapter 1

Introduction

1.1 AIM OF THE STUDY

Compared with the 1970s, the relative position of households with children had deteriorated sharply in Ireland by the late 1980s, as analysed in detail in Nolan and Farrell's (1990) study for the Combat Poverty Agency. Children then faced a much higher risk than adults of being in a poor household. The relative position of children versus adults also worsened in a number of other industrialised countries around that time, but the extent of child income poverty in Ireland was exceptionally high. The macro-economic environment in Ireland has been very different since then, with stagnation replaced by economic growth, with this growth reaching record levels since 1994. How have children fared in that very different setting?

This study for the Combat Poverty Agency uses household survey data to explore in depth the evolution of child poverty in Ireland since the late 1980s, and to put it in a comparative perspective. It aims to identify the main factors producing poverty for Irish children and how these have been changing over time. It also brings out the importance of going beyond household income in monitoring child welfare, by employing and developing other indicators at the level of the household and the child him or herself. The study is intended among other things to contribute to the on-going development of the National Anti Poverty Stategy in this crucial area.

1.2 CONTENT OF THE STUDY

The household survey data on which this study primarily relies is drawn from the 1994 and 1997 rounds of the Living in Ireland Survey, the Irish element of the European Community House-hold Panel survey. The overall extent and nature of poverty in Ireland based on these sources has been analysed in Callan *et al* (1996) and Callan, *et al* (1999) respectively, but here we em-ploy them with a specific focus on child poverty. In Chapter 2, these surveys are used to provide an up-dated picture of the extent of relative income poverty for Irish children, and to compare this with the earlier results available for 1987, 1980 and 1973 analysed in depth in Nolan and Farrell (1990).

Chapter 3 seeks to put such relative income poverty rates for Irish children in comparative perspective. It draws on a variety of data sources to see whether Ireland is unusual in its level of child income poverty. In particular, it investigates whether ear-lier findings suggesting that Ireland had a particularly high level of child income poverty still applied in the mid-1990s.

Chapter 4 then returns to relative income poverty in Ireland. By looking at the types of household in which children below relative income poverty lines live, and how this was changing up to 1997, it aims pin-point the factors at work behind the way these poverty rates have evolved for children versus adults to. In focuses in particular on the role of falling unemployment and the relationship between social welfare rates and average in-comes.

Chapter 5 is concerned with what non-monetary indicators of deprivation can tell us about the households in which children live. It brings out the fact that relative income poverty rates provide a rather partial picture in the situation of rapid growth experienced by Ireland in recent years. The combined income and deprivation measure of poverty, adopted in the National Anti-Poverty Strategy's global poverty reduction target, is used to assess trends in the situation of children versus adults.

One reason that it is important to go beyond current income in assessing living standards and poverty is that income levels may vary for individuals and families from one year to the next. By directly exploring the dynamics of income and of child income poverty, one can see how much movement there is in and out of income poverty. Chapter 6 begins such an analysis for Irish children, drawing on material prepared as part of a UNI-CEF project on the dynamics of child poverty in industrialised countries. Non-monetary indicators of deprivation are also used to help in assessing the implications of income poverty dynamics for the living standards of households with children.

These non-monetary indicators were designed to measure the extent and nature of deprivation at the level of the household, but do not serve as direct measures of living standards or deprivation for the children themselves. The assumption is made that the pooling of resources within the household equalises living standards and poverty risk for all household members. The situation where children are in poverty because of insufficient sharing of resources within the household will not be captured, either with conventional income measures or with the deprivation indicators we have available. Chapter 7 looks at the potential non-monetary deprivation indicators have for capturing the living standards of children, and discusses more broadly some issues relating to the measurement and monitoring of child well being.

Finally, Chapter 8 brings together the main findings of the study, discusses how the continuation of rapid economic growth since 1997 may have affected the extent and nature of child poverty in Ireland, and brings out key issues for policy in terms of child income support.

Chapter 2

Trends in Relative Income Poverty for Irish Children

2.1. INTRODUCTION

Nolan and Farrell's (1990) study on child poverty for the Combat Poverty Agency showed that, compared with the early 1970s, the relative position of households with children had deteriorated sharply in Ireland by the late 1980s. Children then faced a much higher risk than adults of being in a household below relative income poverty lines. The dramatic increase in unemployment during the 1980s was seen to be the principal factor behind this worrying trend.

A decade later, economic growth had accelerated to an unprecedented extent and unemployment had fallen sharply. Against that background, this chapter uses household survey data for 1994 and 1997 to present an up-dated picture of the extent of relative income poverty for Irish children. Later chapters put these figures in comparative perspective, analyse in depth the factors underlying the observed trends, and incorporate non-income as well as income information in assessing recent developments in child poverty. In this chapter we simply describe how relative income poverty rates for children have evolved, in the context of the corresponding poverty rates for adults and for households.

2.2. THE DATA

The data on which we primarily draw in this chapter come from two waves of the Living in Ireland Survey, the Irish element of the European Community Household Panel (ECHP). The 1994 Living in Ireland Survey was the first wave, and used the Electoral Register as the sampling frame. This survey obtained information for 4,048 households, a response rate of 62.5 per cent of valid addresses contacted. To ensure the representativeness of the data, the sample has been re-weighted using weights derived from sources such as the Census of Population and the Labour Force Survey, in terms of number of adults in the household, number at work in the household, socio-economic group, age and location. The representativeness of the data after re-weighting has been validated by comparison with information from external sources on a variety of other dimensions. Results from this survey on household poverty have been published in Callan *et al* (1996), which also contains a comprehensive description of the survey itself.

The second data set is from 1997, the fourth wave of the Living in Ireland Survey. The aim of the panel survey is to follow all individuals in the Wave 1 sample, and conduct household and individual interviews, as long as the person still lives in a private or collective[1] household within the EU. The follow-up rules for the survey mean that new households are included in each wave where a sample person moved to another household. The wave-on-wave attrition rate in the Irish panel was quite high: of the original 14,585 individuals in the 1994 sample, only 63 per cent (9,208) were still in completed Wave 4 households, with another 805 individuals having joined the sample at some point in the intervening years. The main reason for

---

[1] Collective households are private households containing numerous "sub-households" and include boarding or lodging houses and army barracks, but not include institutions such as hospitals, nursing homes, convents or prisons.

household non-response was refusal (ranging from 9 per cent of the eligible sample in Wave 2 to 6 per cent in Wave 4). Among the newly-generated households, difficulties in obtaining forwarding addresses for those who moved also contributed to the non-response rate.

Given relatively high sample attrition rates, it was important to carefully check whether any biases were introduced by attrition related to characteristics of households, such as size, location, economic status and income. These checks were conducted in the course of devising longitudinal weights for the data in Waves 2 to 4, using information on the households and individuals from the previous wave's interviews as well as using external information. In general, the results are encouraging, suggesting that the overall impact of attrition on the sample structure is slight. In particular, there was no evidence that households with specific characteristics related to the measurement of poverty (in terms of income or deprivation levels or social security recipiency in Wave 1) have been selectively lost from the sample. A comprehensive description of the 1997 Survey, the re-weighting procedure and these validation exercises is in Callan *et al* (1999).

Eurostat, the statistical office of the EU, has sought to harmonise the core questionnaires employed in each country participating in the ECHP in terms of structure, content and interpretation. As well as income, a range of questions about a range of non-monetary indicators of life-style and deprivation were included, which as we shall see prove particularly useful in assessing the living standards of households. The Living in Ireland Survey contains this core, but also various additional modules and questions. In terms of income, Eurostat's main concern was with disposable income (i.e., gross income minus compulsory deductions for tax and Social Insurance contributions) in the calendar year before the interview. In addition, the Irish version of the questionnaire also collected details on current income receipts from these sources, allowing both current and annual income to be measured. The Irish survey also included a broader range of non-monetary indicators and subjective questions, covering for example psychological distress.

In providing a longer-term perspective back to the early 1970s, we also draw on three other surveys, which served as the basis for the analysis of child income poverty up to the late 1980s in Nolan and Farrell (1990). For 1987, results are available from the household survey carried out by the ESRI in that year, employed in the extensive programme of research on poverty in Ireland summarised in Nolan & Callan (1994). For 1980 and 1973 results were derived from the 1973 and 1980 Household Budget Surveys carried out by the CSO. (This analysis of the micro-data from the budget surveys was kindly facilitated by the CSO). Detailed descriptions of these surveys can be found in Callan *et al* (1989) and the CSO (1984) respectively. These three years are the only years before 1994 for which such household surveys, gathering detailed income data on a large representative national sample, were carried out in Ireland.

2.3. MEASURING RELATIVE INCOME POVERTY

A relative standard for measuring poverty in developed countries is by now widely though not universally accepted. The definition of poverty employed in the National Anti-Poverty Strategy recently adopted by the Irish government is typical:

> People are living in poverty if their income and resources (material, cultural and social) are so inadequate as to preclude them from having a standard of living which is regarded as acceptable by Irish society generally. As a result of inadequate income and resources people may be excluded and marginalised from participating in activities which are considered the norm for other people in society. (NAPS 1997, p. 3).

In actually implementing such a definition to measure the extent of poverty, the most common approach has been to define a poverty line in terms of income, and regard those with incomes below the line as poor. One way to set that income poverty line is, then, to take it as a proportion of average income, adjusted for the greater needs of larger families, and this general approach has been widely adopted in comparative studies of poverty across industrialised countries. (Some studies do of course apply a common real income standard over time or across countries: we mention the implications of such an approach in the Irish case below.) While Irish research on poverty has sought to go beyond reliance on income alone, as we discuss in detail in Chapter 5, a great deal can be learned from the application of relative income poverty lines and that is where we begin.

We therefore concentrate in this chapter on income poverty, measured vis-à-vis relative income poverty lines. We follow conventional poverty measurement practice in adopting the household as the income- and resources-sharing unit throughout this study, treating all members of a particular household as having the same standard of living. Some analysis of the situation of individuals within households has been undertaken using ESRI survey data, particularly as it affects women (see Rottman (1994) and Cantillon and Nolan (1998). Intra-household distributional issues, including the implications for children, are being explored in a related project currently under way for the Combat Poverty Agency which will be discussed in Chapter 6 below. For the purpose of this study, though, an individual is poor if he or she lives in a poor household, and this applies equally to children and adults.

Again following conventional practice, equivalence scales are used to adjust household income for the differences in "needs" associated with differing size and composition. To assess the sensitivity of the findings, a variety of scales is employed here as in previous work, and a detailed description of these scales and their derivation is given in Callan *et al* (1996). The first scale was derived from Irish social security rates paid in the late 1980s. Where the first adult in a household is given the value 1, this gives each additional adult a value of 0.66 and each child a value of 0.33 in calculating the total number of "equivalent adults" in the household. The second scale, often employed in UK research, gives each additional adult a value of 0.6 and each child 0.4. The third scale, often called the "OECD scale", attributes to each additional adult a value of 0.7 and each child 0.5. In calculating these scales, we follow Hagenaars *et al*'s study for Eurostat (1994) in defining children as those aged under 14 years of age. Equivalent or equivalised household income is then total income divided by the number of equivalent adults in the household. Although this age cut-off is employed in constructing equivalence scales, we also look in the course of the study at "children" under 16 or under 18 years of age.

In constructing relative income poverty lines, a number of other choices have to be made. One is whether the mean or the median income is to be used in deriving those lines. The mean can be seen as preferable in being more generally understood, but it may be highly sensitive to a small number of very high incomes, unlike the median. We use mean income as the basis for the main results presented here, because it is not now possible to derive median-based poverty lines from the Household Budget Survey going back to 1973. However, we also examine whether more recent trends are affected by the use of the median rather than the mean.

The mean itself can be calculated either by averaging (equivalised) income over households, or by calculating the average over individuals having attributing the equivalised income of the household to each individual in it. A case can be made for either approach and here we present results for both.

We use three cut-offs — 40, 50 and 60 per cent of mean income — in order to test the sensitivity of conclusions to the precise location of the poverty line.

2.4 Trends in Relative Income Poverty for Children

We now look at overall trends in relative income poverty in Ireland over the whole period from 1973 to 1997, and at the pattern for children versus adults. In this section we present results for relative income lines based on the mean rather than the median, and averaged across households rather than persons; in the next section we look at the difference made by alternative approaches to deriving the relative income lines.

Table 2.1 shows the percentage of households falling below the 50 per cent relative income poverty line for the years 1973, 1980, 1987, 1994 and 1997, for the three equivalence scales, and then the percentage of individuals living in those households. We see that the percentage of households below the 50 per cent line fell between 1973 and 1987 for each equivalence scale, then rose to 1994 with the first two scales but continued to fall with the third one. Between 1994 and 1997, the proportion of households below this line rose with all three scales. The percentage of persons in households falling below the 50 per cent line rose slightly between 1973 and 1980, more rapidly between 1980 and 1987, and continued to rise to 1994 and again to 1997 with all three equivalence scales — households below these lines are larger than average. The relative poverty rates for persons in 1997 on this basis are considerably higher than in 1973 with all three scales.

Table 2.1: Percentage of Households and Persons below 50 Per Cent Relative Income Poverty Line with Alternative Equivalence Scales, Ireland 1973–97

	1973 HBS	1980 HBS	1987 ESRI	1994 LII	1997 LII
Equivalence scale	*% of households below 50% line*				
1/0.66/0.33	18.3	16.8	16.3	19.1	21.8
1/0.6/0.4	18.8	17.6	17.1	20.5	23.0
1/0.7/0.5	18.9	17.2	17.6	18.4	20.3
Equivalence scale	*% of persons in these households*				
1/0.66/0.33	15.5	16.2	18.9	21.0	21.7
1/0.6/0.4	16.8	17.4	20.1	21.8	22.6
1/0.7/0.5	18.6	19.2	21.8	23.0	23.3

Do relative income poverty lines set at 40 per cent or 60 per cent of mean equivalent income show the same picture as the 50 per cent line? Table 2.2 shows the percentage of persons living in households below these relative income poverty lines, focusing on the 1/0.66/0.33 equivalence scale. Of course, very different numbers of households and persons are below these lines in any year: about 7-10 per cent of persons were in households below the 40 per cent line and between 25-35 per cent were in households below 60 per cent of mean income, compared with the 15-22 per cent in households below the 50 per cent line. In terms of trends over time, there is no consistent pattern with the 40 per cent line, but there is a consistent increase from one survey to the next in the percentage of persons in households falling below the 60 per cent line. As detailed elsewhere, this is generally but not invariably also the case with the other equivalence scales we have employed (see Callan *et al* 1996, 1999).

Table 2.2: Percentage of Persons in Households Below Alternative Relative Income Poverty Lines, Ireland 1973–97

	1973	1980	1987	1994	1997
	*% of persons in households below line**				
40 per cent line	7.6	8.5	6.8	6.9	9.9
50 per cent line	15.5	16.2	18.9	21.0	21.7
60 per cent line	25.5	26.7	29.8	33.9	35.0

* Equivalence scale 1/0.66/0.33

Against this background, how have children fared? Table 2.3 shows the percentage of children (defined for the present as under 14 years of age) and adults living in households below each of the relative income lines, with the 1/0.66/0.33 equivalence scale, in each year. From 1973 to 1994, the risk of relative income poverty for children increased at all three cut-offs. Between 1994 and 1997, however, the risk for children rose with the lowest relative line but fell with the 50 and 60 per cent lines. In Chapter 3 we explore the factors underlying these trends, including the contrast between the pattern shown by the lowest line versus the other two thresholds between 1994 and 1997.

Table 2.3: Risks of Relative Income Poverty for Children and Adults, Ireland 1973–97

	1973 HBS	1980 HBS	1987 ESRI	1994 LII	1997 LII
	*% of children below relative income line**				
40% line	8.1	10.1	7.6	8.0	13.2
50% line	16.2	18.5	25.5	29.5	26.0
60% line	27.5	29.5	37.8	40.2	37.2
	*% of adults below relative income line**				
40% line	7.4	7.7	6.5	6.6	9.1
50% line	15.1	15.2	16.1	18.2	20.5
60% line	24.4	25.4	26.5	31.8	34.4

* Equivalence scale 1/0.66/0.33.

By comparison, we see that the risks for adults are much less volatile over the whole period. The risk for adults was broadly unchanged between 1973 and 1987, and then increased at the 50 per cent and 60 per cent lines to 1994, and at all three lines from there to 1997. In terms of the position of children versus adults, then, children had a slightly higher risk in 1973, but by 1987 a much more substantial gap had opened up, with children at much higher risk using the 50 per cent or 60 per cent line. This gap persisted in 1994. However, since the risk for adults rose but that for children fell between 1994 and 1997 with the 50 per cent and 60 per cent lines, the gap between risks for children versus adults narrowed significantly over these three years. With the 40 per cent line, on the other hand, the risk for children not only rose, it did so more rapidly than for adults and produced a widening gap.

How much do child poverty rates on this basis vary depending on the equivalence scale employed? Table 2.4 shows for 1987, 1994 and 1997 the percentage of children in households below the 50 per cent relative income line with the three sets of equivalence scales described earlier. We see that the child poverty rate is indeed rather sensitive to the scale used. The other two scales now used both incorporate higher "costs for children" than the 1/0.66/0.33 scale, and show higher child poverty rates. With the so-called OECD (1/0.7/0.5) scale, about 32 per cent of children were in households below half average equivalent income in 1997, compared with 26 per cent with the 1/0.66/0.33 scale. However, the overall trend between 1973 and 1997 we saw with the 1/0.66/0.33 scale and the 50 per cent poverty line — of rising child poverty rates to 1994 followed by a decline to 1997 — is also found with each of the other two scales.

Table 2.4: Percentage of Children below 50 Per Cent Relative Income Poverty Line, Alternative Equivalence Scales, 1973–97

	1973	1980	1987	1994	1997
	% of children below 50% line				
1/0.66/0.33	16.2	18.5	25.5	29.5	26.0
1/0.6/0.4	19.9	21.3	29.2	31.7	28.7
1/0.7/0.5	23.5	24.8	32.7	35.2	32.1

2.5 CHILDREN AND RELATIVE INCOME POVERTY WITH ALTERNATIVE APPROACHES

The results presented in the previous section are based on relative income poverty lines constructed in a particular way: the poverty lines are derived as proportions of mean rather than median equivalised household income, and that mean is calculated by averaging over households rather than persons. These represent alternative valid approaches — one is not unambiguously preferable to the other. It is particularly important then to know whether what may appear to be innocuous technical choices make a significant difference to the results. We therefore look in this section first at alternative ways of deriving mean-based lines, and then at the use of the median rather than the mean: these analyses can only be carried out from 1987 on.

Table 2.5 shows for 1987, 1994 and 1997 the percentage of persons falling below the 50 per cent relative income line, using mean equivalent income averaged over individuals as a benchmark, and with each of the three equivalence scales. These poverty lines turn out to be about 2-3 percentage points lower than those for persons in Table 2.1. Furthermore, comparing 1997 with 1994 no longer shows a consistent increase in the percentage of persons below the relative income line. The method of averaging does clearly matter, then, and it is important to ensure consistency in making comparisons over time or across countries.

Table 2.5: Percentage of Persons Below 50% Income Poverty Line (Based on Income Averaged Across Individuals), 1987, 1994 and 1997

	1987	1994	1997
	% of persons below 50% line		
1/0.66/0.33	17.4	18.6	19.8
1/0.6/0.4	17.9	19.6	19.3
1/0.7/0.5	18.6	19.2	19.6

As far as children are concerned, if we average across persons rather than households, Table 2.6 shows that the poverty rates for children in 1997 are about 2 percentage points lower than those shown in Table 2.3 — 24 per cent rather than 26 per cent are below half average income, for example. However, the same changes in the gap between adults and children — widening with the 40 per cent line but narrowing with the 50 per cent and 60 per cent ones — are seen between 1994 and 1997 as when income was averaged over households.

Table 2.6: *Risks of Relative Income Poverty for Adults and Children, Ireland 1987–97 (Income Averaged Across Individuals)*

	1987 ESRI	1994 LII	1997 LII
	% of children below relative income line*		
40% line	6.5	6.2	11.5
50% line	24.0	26.4	24.3
60% line	35.5	38.2	34.9
	% of adults below relative income line*		
40% line	5.8	5.5	8.5
50% line	14.7	16.1	18.6
60% line	24.2	29.3	32.2

* Equivalence scale 1/0.66/0.33.

The relative poverty lines used so far are based on proportions of average equivalent income. As mentioned earlier, the mean may be quite sensitive to a small number of very high incomes reported at the top of the distribution. It is therefore also valuable to examine poverty lines derived as proportions of median income, since the median is not affected by outliers in the same way. Because income distributions are skewed, the median invariably lies below the mean, so this also entails using lower poverty lines. Callan *et al* (1996) reported that in 1994, the percentage of persons falling below 40, 50 and 60 per cent of median equivalised income was about 5 per cent, 15 per cent and 26 per cent respectively. Callan *et al* (1999) found that in 1997, the corresponding figures were about 9–10 per cent, 17–19 per cent and 27–29 per cent depending on the equivalence scale used — suggesting once again that the extent of relative income poverty was, if anything, higher in 1997 than in 1994.

Here our concern is with the position of children. Table 2.7 therefore shows the percentage of children and of adults falling below relative income lines derived as proportions of the median rather than the mean. Since few fall below 40 per cent of the median, as in Callan *et al* (1999) we look at 50 per cent, 60 per cent and 70 per cent of the median. (We use here the median of the distribution of equivalised income across individuals rather than households, though this in fact makes much less difference with the median than it does with the mean). We see once again a very similar pattern to that shown by the mean-based relative poverty lines in Table 2.6. In particular, there is little or no gap between adults and children with the lowest line in 1987 or 1994 but one has emerged by 1997, whereas with the middle and highest lines there is a pronounced gap in 1987 and 1994 but a significant narrowing between 1994 and 1997.

Child Poverty in Ireland

Table 2.7: Risks of Relative Income Poverty for Adults and Children, Ireland 1987–97 (Median Income Among Individuals)

	1987 ESRI	1994 LII	1997 LII
	*% of children below relative income line**		
50% line	8.0	6.6	13.1
60% line	24.0	23.5	23.9
70% line	33.1	34.3	33.6
	*% of adults below relative income line**		
50% line	6.7	5.6	9.1
60% line	14.6	13.3	18.0
70% line	21.9	24.1	29.2

* Equivalence scale 1/0.66/0.33.

We now turn to one final issue in this chapter. Relative income lines tell only part of the story in terms of income poverty, and it is also relevant to look at income standards held fixed in real terms over time. In this context, Callan *et al* (1996, 1999) have employed an illustrative standard set at 60 per cent of average equivalent income in 1987 and up-rated in line with prices rather than average incomes to 1994 and 1997 respectively. They found a sharp decline both from 1987 to 1994 and from 1994 to 1997 in the percentage of persons falling below such a "real income" line. In 1987, about one-third of all persons in the sample were below 60 per cent of mean equivalised income. By 1997, only about 11 per cent were below that line uprated by the increase in prices. What about children? We saw in Table 2.3 that the percentage of children in households below that line was 38 per cent. Table 2.8 shows that this had fallen to 25 per cent by 1994, and to 17 per cent by 1997. The corresponding figure for adults fell from 26 per cent to 11 per cent. This particular poverty line representing fixed purchasing power thus gives a very different picture of trends over the decade to those framed in purely relative terms — which is not surprising when average incomes grew so rapidly in real terms. It does, however, still show substantial persisting disadvantage for children compared to adults. We return to the impact of increasing average incomes in Chapter 5, when we explore what non-monetary indicators of deprivation show about changing living standards.

Table 2.8: Percentage of Children and Adults Below 1987 Real Income Standard, 1994 and 1997

	1987	1994	1997
	*% of children below "real" income line**		
1987 60% line	37.8	25.1	17.2
	*% of adults below "real" income line**		
1987 60% line	26.5	15.1	11.4

* Equivalence scale 1/0.66/0.33.

2.6 CONCLUSIONS

This chapter has shown that from 1973 to 1994, the risk of relative income poverty for children increased in Ireland, consistently across different relative income thresholds. Between 1994 and 1997, however, the risk for children rose if 40 per cent of the mean is used as the relative income line but fell with lines set at 50 per cent or 60 per cent of the mean.

The corresponding poverty risks for adults were much less volatile over the whole period. The risk for adults was broadly unchanged between 1973 and 1987, and then increased at the 50 per cent and 60 per cent lines to 1994, and at all three lines from there to 1997. In terms of the position of children versus adults, then, children had a slightly higher risk in 1973, but by 1987 a much more substantial gap had opened up, with children at much higher risk using the 50 per cent or 60 per cent line. This gap persisted in 1994. However, since the risk for adults rose but that for children fell between 1994 and 1997 with the 50 per cent and 60 per cent lines, the gap between risks for children versus adults narrowed significantly over these three years. With the 40 per cent line, on the other hand, the risk for children not only rose, it did so more rapidly than for adults and produced a widening gap.

Alternative formulations of relative income lines, based on averaging across persons rather than households or on the median rather than the mean, show a similar pattern. An income standard set at 60 per cent of the mean in 1987 and up-rated only in line with prices, by contrast, shows marked falls in the poverty rate for both children and adults since then. It does, however, still show substantial persisting disadvantage for children compared to adults.

We explore in some detail in subsequent chapters the factors underlying these trends for Ireland, and go beyond income poverty to incorporate non-monetary indicators of deprivation into the picture. First, though, we put the Irish situation in a comparative context by looking in the next chapter at relative income poverty for children in Ireland compared with other industrialised countries.

Chapter 3

Relative Income Poverty for Irish Children in Comparative Perspective

3.1 INTRODUCTION

In the previous chapter we applied what is now a commonly used approach to measuring poverty in industrialised countries, namely relative income poverty lines, to data for Ireland. This allowed us to see the extent of relative income poverty affecting Irish children and how that has been changing over time. In this chapter we seek to provide a comparative perspective on child poverty in Ireland. How does child poverty in Ireland, measured in this way, compare with other industrialised countries? Such cross-country comparisons of poverty and income distribution in the past have been bedevilled by differences in the underlying data or in the way the measures are actually produced. Here we draw on a number of studies published in recent years, which have aimed at a high degree of comparability in terms of definitions, measures and sources. We begin with several studies relating to the 1980s, and then turn to the more up-to-date information available for the 1990s.

3.2 COMPARATIVE DATA ON CHILD POVERTY IN THE 1980s

The statistical office of the European Communities, Eurostat, has sponsored a number of comparative studies of poverty across the member states. The one carried out by the Institute of Social

Studies in The Hague (Institute of Social Studies Advisory Service, 1990) presented figures for around 1980 and around 1985, based on analysis of the household budget survey data. For Ireland, the data used in this study came from the Household Budget Surveys carried out by the CSO in 1980 and 1987. Household expenditure per equivalent adult was used as the welfare indicator, rather than income. The equivalence scale employed gave a value of 1 to the first adult in each household, 0.7 to each other adult, and 0.5 to each child (defined as aged under 14). Poverty thresholds set at 40 and 50 per cent of mean equivalised expenditure, averaged across households, were employed.

Table 3.1 shows the percentage of children in households below 40 per cent and 50 per cent of the mean for their own country, taken from this study, for 1980. The results show Ireland having a relatively high rate of child income poverty at that time, along with Greece, Spain, France and the UK, with only Portugal having a much higher rate. Over one-fifth of Irish children were in households below the 50 per cent line.

Table 3.1: Percentage of Children Below 40% and 50% of National Average Equivalent Expenditure, 1980

	Children (under 14) below Poverty Line	
	% below 40%	*% below 50% line*
Belgium	2.4	8.0
Denmark	3.7	8.7
Germany	5.1	11.5
Greece	11.4	20.7
Spain	12.9	22.1
France	10.7	20.7
Ireland	12.6	22.4
Italy	10.5	16.1
Netherlands	4.7	13.1
Portugal	24.5	36.2
UK	9.1	20.1

Source: ISSAS 1990, Table 4.2, p. 32

The corresponding results for the mid-1980s, also presented in the ISSAS study, are shown in Table 3.2. Child poverty rates for Ireland were shown to have risen markedly since 1980, which is consistent with the trend we have seen in Chapter 2. Almost 28 per cent of all Irish children were in households below the 50 per cent line by the mid-1980s (actually 1987), and this meant that among the member states Ireland had a child poverty rate second only to Portugal's.

Table 3.2: Percentage of Children Below 40% and 50% of National Average Equivalent Expenditure, 1985

	Children (under 14) below Poverty Line	
	% below 40% line	*% below 50% line*
Belgium	1.7	6.7
Denmark	4.0	9.1
Germany	5.9	13.7
Greece	9.7	18.9
Spain	12.2	20.2
France	10.4	19.5
Ireland	15.7	27.9
Italy	9.0	15.1
Netherlands	5.5	17.7
Portugal	24.7	36.6
UK	13.5	24.0

Source: ISSAS 1990, Table 4.5, p. 35 and Annex B, Table B.8, p. 80.

As well as relative poverty lines constructed using average expenditure in the country in question, the ISSAS study also looked at Community-wide standards. In other words, the equivilised expenditure of households was compared not only with half the average in their own country, but also with half the average across the Community as a whole. This would of course represent a poverty standard that was lower for richer member states but higher for the poorer ones — then including Ireland

— than their own national average. Table 3.3 shows the percentage of children in each country below half that Community-wide average in 1980 and 1985. We see that in 1980, one-quarter of Irish children were in households below that standard, which was higher than most other member states but lower than Spain, Greece and Portugal. By the mid-1980s, however, the Irish rate had risen very sharply indeed to 35 per cent. This reflected the fact that over the period not only did purely relative poverty rates for Irish children rise, but mean income or expenditure stagnated in Ireland when the Community average was increasing. As a result, in the mid-1980s Ireland had a higher child poverty rate measured against this Community-wide standard than even Spain and Greece, with Portugal the only member state with a higher rate (though this was very much higher).

Table 3.3: Percentage of Children Below 50% of Average Equivalent Expenditure in the European Community, 1980 and 1985

	Children (under 14) below 50% Line	
	1980	*1985*
Belgium	3.1	2.1
Denmark	4.3	3.1
Germany	7.9	9.8
Greece	28.1	21.6
Spain	32.1	33.6
France	17.8	15.0
Ireland	25.9	35.0
Italy	17.1	13.4
Netherlands	5.0	7.1
Portugal	70.3	71.2
UK	20.4	21.0
Average	**19.7**	**19.4**

Source: ISSAS 1990, Table 3.3, p. 25 and Annex B, Table B.6, p. 79.

Following up on the ISSAS study, Eurostat commissioned research by Hagenaars, de Vos and Zaidi (1994). They sought to use data for the late 1980s, and to explore the impact of alternative technical choices in constructing relative income poverty lines, through direct analysis of micro-data from the household budget surveys. As far as children are concerned, they represent the percentage in households falling below 50 per cent of mean equivalised expenditure in their own country, the same poverty standard and measure as employed in Tables 3.1 and 3.2. The figures differ from Table 3.2 either because they refer to a different year or, as in the case of Ireland (where the 1987 Household Budget Survey is again the source), because the micro-data was employed. We see that Ireland once again has the second-highest child poverty rate in the Community, with Portugal now only marginally higher.

Table 3.4: Percentage of Children Below 50% of National Average Equivalent Expenditure, Late-1980s

	Children (under 14) below 50% of Average Equivalent Expenditures
	%
Belgium	6.2
Denmark	3.3
Germany	14.4
Greece	15.0
Spain	16.8
France	16.0
Ireland	21.0
Italy	19.5
Luxembourg	11.4
Netherlands	4.3
Portugal	22.3
UK	18.5

Source: Hagenaars et al (1994), Table 3, p. 9.

The final study dealing with the 1980s on which we draw is by Bradbury and Jantti (1999). Unlike the other studies we have discussed so far, they employ data in the Luxembourg Income Study (LIS) database, and also differ methodologically in a number of respects. Their results are of particular value in the current context in going beyond the European Community to cover for example, the US, Canada, Australia and some of the transition economies of central and eastern Europe (though Portugal is not now included because it is not in the LIS). As far as methodology is concerned, they focus on income rather than expenditure. Both country-specific relative income poverty lines — based on proportions of the median rather than the mean — and a common standard, namely the US official poverty line (converted using Purchasing Power Parities), are used. An equivalence scale broadly similar to the "OECD" scale, though constructed in a different way, is employed and the median is derived from the distribution of equivalised income across persons rather than households. Table 3.5 shows some of their principal results.

We see first that among European Community members, Ireland once again has a relatively high child poverty rate when the country-specific standard is used. However, both Italy and the UK are now shown to have higher rates. This reflects the fact that data for many of the countries covered, including Italy and the UK, is for the early- to mid-1990s but the Irish data in the LIS database still refer to 1987, as well as the use of the median rather than the mean. Child poverty rates on this basis are also higher in Australia and Canada than in Ireland, while that for the USA is very much higher. Denmark, Norway, and Sweden, on the other hand, have child poverty rates under 5 per cent on this basis. Using the common standard of the US official poverty line gives a rather different picture, of course. Differences across countries in average income levels now play a major role, and more than half all Irish children were below such a line in 1987.

Table 3.5: Percentage of Children Below 50% of Median Equivalent Income and US Official Poverty Line, Industrialised Countries, late 1980s to early 1990s

		Children (under 18) below Poverty Line	
		50% of median	*US official poverty line*
Belgium	1992	6.1	7.9
Denmark	1992	5.9	4.6
Germany	1994	11.6	12.4
Spain	1990	13.1	47.3
France	1989	9.8	17.3
Luxembourg	1994	6.3	1.1
Ireland	1987	14.8	54.4
Italy	1995	21.2	38.1
Netherlands	1991	8.4	10.0
UK	1995	21.3	28.6
Australia	1994	17.1	20.7
Austria	1987	5.6	5.4
Canada	1994	16.0	9.0
Finland	1991	3.4	2.6
Norway	1995	4.5	2.8
Sweden	1992	3.7	3.7
Switzerland	1982	6.3	1.6
USA	1994	26.3	18.5
Czech Republic	1992	1.8	85.1
Hungary	1994	11.5	90.6
Poland	1992	14.2	90.9
Slovakia	1992	2.2	95.2
Russia	1995	26.6	98.0

Source: Bradbury and Jantti (1999), Table 3.3, p. 18.

3.3 COMPARATIVE DATA ON CHILD POVERTY IN THE 1990S

While the results discussed in the previous section are very valuable, they suffer from two shortcomings in terms of providing an up-to-date comparative picture against which to see relative income poverty for Irish children. The first is that the Irish data relate to 1980 and 1987; the second is that the databases employed come originally from different national surveys, and despite strenuous efforts to harmonise definitions etc. there may still be areas where this poses problems. For both these reasons, the fact that since 1994 Eurostat has organised the European Community Household Panel Survey, being carried out in most of the EU member states on a harmonised basis, represents a significant step forward. Eurostat (1999) has recently produced figures from the second wave of the ECHP, which allow comparisons to be made of the extent of relative income poverty in the participating member states. The income concept is annual disposable income in the previous calendar year (in this case 1994), and equivalisation employs the "modified OECD" scale, attributing 1 to the first adult in the household, 0.5 to each other adult, and 0.3 to each child (aged under 14). The results are not directly comparable with those for Ireland in 1987 discussed in the previous section, or those for 1994 and 1997 discussed in the previous chapter, because of differences in the income measure. They do, however, allow a harmonised and more up-to-date comparative picture to be seen.

The figures presented relate first to the percentage below half the average income in the country in question (averaged over persons). For this purpose children under 16 are identified, and the poverty rates for this age group are shown in Table 3.6. We see that 30 per cent of Irish children are below that line. Ireland in fact has the highest rate of child poverty, measured in this way, of any of the member states included in the survey. Only Portugal and the UK have a child poverty rate nearly as high, and in many of the member countries the rate is half Ireland's or below. Eurostat has also produced corresponding figures for the percentage falling below 60 per cent of the median rather than 50 per cent of the mean. These are also shown in Table 3.6, and we can see that they show very much the same picture.

Table 3.6: Percentage of Children Below 50% Relative Income Poverty Line in European Union Countries, 1994

	Children (under 16) below Poverty Line	
	% below 50% of mean	*% below 60% of median*
Belgium	15	18
Denmark	5	6
Germany	18	22
Greece	14	16
Spain	22	22
France	15	17
Ireland	30	28
Italy	20	22
Luxembourg	19	19
Netherlands	10	12
Austria	18	21
Portugal	27	26
UK	28	28
Average	**19**	**21**

Source: Eurostat (1999), Table C1.0, p. 60-61 and Table C1.7, p. 98-99

The Eurostat study does not apply a common European income standard across the member states. In terms of income per capita, by 1994 Ireland's relative position had improved compared with the late 1980s. Nonetheless, mean equivalised income in Ireland was still below the average for all the member states. Applying such a common standard would thus increase the measured poverty rate in Ireland compared with a purely relative line, though by less than in Spain, Greece or especially Portugal where mean equivalised income is lower.

Ireland's poor showing compared with other European countries in terms of relative income poverty for children was a significant factor leading the United Nations Committee on the Rights of the Child to recommend that the Irish government adopt a programme to eradicate child poverty as a priority.[1] While these are the most recent comparative figures available at present, it is important to note the implications of the fact that they relate to 1994. Since then, Ireland has experienced a remarkable economic boom, and we saw in the previous chapter that Irish relative income poverty rates for children had come down by 1997, the latest date for which national survey information is currently available. While a direct comparison with the numbers presented here cannot be made due to differences in the income measure, it is likely that the Irish rate shown in Table 3.6 was down by several percentage points by 1997. As discussed later on, there is also reason to believe that a mix of factors broadly similar to the 1994–97 period has been operating since 1997, with unemployment falling further but social welfare lagging behind other incomes, so a further decline in child income poverty rates may have occurred. Without knowing what has happened elsewhere it is difficult to assess the implications for Ireland's ranking vis-à-vis other EU member states. It does seem likely however that more up-to-date figures would show Ireland as one of a group (including Portugal and the UK) with high relative income poverty rates for children, rather than as the country with the highest rate in the Union.

Why do these countries have such high child poverty rates, measured in this way? While unemployment was certainly still a major factor underlying child poverty in Ireland in 1994, it was

---

[1] United Nations Information Service. *Committee on Rights of Child Concludes Consideration of Report by Ireland*. Press Release. 13 January 1998.

clearly not the only one. A number of factors can be advanced at this stage that apply both to Ireland and the UK, to be investigated in some depth for Ireland in the following chapters. The first is that unemployment does not convey the whole story as far as access by households to income from work is concerned. To bring this out, Table 3.7 draws on a study by the OECD of the extent to which households with children in different countries have no-one in employment. Using figures for 1996, it distinguishes households with one, two and three or more working age adults, in each case containing at least one child aged 14 or under, and shows the percentage having no one in employment. We see that within each of the three categories, Ireland actually had the highest percentage with no one in employment of any of the countries covered. Indeed, the Irish figures were about twice the average. The UK also had a very high proportion in that situation in each group. Unemployment in Ireland has approximately halved since then, but the proportion of households with children and no one in employment must still be relatively high. This reflects both the extent of inactivity among working-age adults (which encompasses not only unemployment but illness and disability, education and working full-time in the home) and the way in which worklessness is concentrated in particular households.

The other factor one would expect to play a major role is the extent and nature of support provided by the state for families with children through the benefit and tax systems. Here, Ireland and the UK again have striking similarities in terms of the structures through which this support is provided, and we will discuss later the level of support and how much impact increasing it might have on relative income poverty rates.

Table 3.7: Percentage of Non-Employment for Working-Age Households with Children, OECD Countries, 1996

	% with No One at Work		
	Single adult with children	Two adults with children	Three or more adults with children
Australia	57.1	9.4	6.6
Austria	23.5	3.3	2.0
Belgium	51.1	6.3	10.0
Canada	48.9	8.2	6.5
Finland	41.8	7.2	5.6
France	34.0	5.9	6.7
Germany	38.0	5.5	4.6
Greece	35.4	3.1	4.2
Ireland	61.2	12.0	11.2
Italy	28.9	6.6	6.7
Luxembourg	29.7	2.1	1.8
Netherlands	55.1	5.7	5.3
Portugal	25.2	2.5	1.8
Spain	39.4	9.0	9.7
UK	60.8	10.7	8.5
USA	34.1	5.7	5.7
Average	**39.7**	**6.0**	**5.5**

Source: OECD (1998), Table 1.7, p. 18.

3.4 CONCLUSIONS

This chapter has presented a range of comparative figures on the extent of relative income poverty for children in industrialised countries. By the late 1980s, Ireland was seen to have a relatively high child poverty rate on this basis compared with other European Community members. More up-to-date figures for 1994 show that Ireland in fact had the highest rate of child poverty, measured in this way, of any of the member states. Only Portugal and the UK had a child poverty rate nearly as high, and in many of the member countries the rate is half Ireland's or below. Other industrialised countries such as Australia, Canada and particularly the USA also had high child poverty rates measured in this way. Applying a common income poverty line across EU or industrialised countries gave a rather different picture, but Ireland in the mid-1990s would still have a relatively high poverty rate on that basis.

The declines in unemployment since the mid-1990s are likely to have improved Ireland's relative ranking but Ireland probably still has a higher relative income poverty rate for children than its EU partners other than the UK and Portugal. In terms of underlying factors, a striking similarity between Ireland and the UK is the high proportion of households with children with no-one in employment — reflecting both high inactivity rates and the concentration of inactivity among certain households. Ireland and the UK also have similar tax and benefit structures for providing income support to families, and we explore in subsequent chapters the impact of these structures and support levels on child poverty in Ireland.

Chapter 4

Understanding Relative Income Poverty Among Irish Children

4.1 INTRODUCTION

To try to understand why so many Irish children find themselves in households below relative income poverty lines, and why this has been changing over time, we now look at the characteristics of these households across a number of dimensions. Having briefly sketched out the changing macroeconomic and policy context in Section 4.2, we look at participation in the paid labour force in Section 4.3 and then at household composition in 4.4. In each case the changing risk and incidence for different types of household with children are charted from 1987 through 1994 and 1997, helping to pin-point key factors at work. In concluding, we draw attention to what may have happened after 1997 as economic growth continued at an unprecedented pace.

4.2 THE MACROECONOMIC AND POLICY BACKGROUND

The central feature of the Irish economy from the 1970s has been exceptionally pronounced fluctuations in economic growth. Following a misplaced fiscal pump-priming in the late 1970s, there was little or no economic growth from 1980 to 1987 as the government struggled to bring the public finances under control. In each of the years from 1987 to 1994, on the other hand, growth in real Gross Domestic Product exceeded both the European Union and OECD average. Economic growth has been even more rapid since then, with GDP increasing by 7-8 per cent per annum — the "Celtic Tiger" phenomenon. Over the 1990s as a whole, Ireland has been one of the fastest growing economies in the OECD. The factors producing this growth are many and the balance between them debated; for an overview and interpretation of the recent Irish growth experience, see, for example, Bradley, FitzGerald, Honohan and Kearney (1997), Barry (1999).

The absence of growth meant that unemployment rose very rapidly during the 1980s, reaching 18 per cent of the labour force by 1987 (as measured in the Labour Force Survey rather than by numbers "signing on" for social welfare). The extent of long-term unemployment was of particular concern, with those unemployed for a year or more accounting for a particularly high proportion of total unemployment in the Irish case. Unemployment proved initially resistant to the renewal of economic growth, still remaining as high as 16 per cent by 1994, but subsequently fell rapidly, down to 11 per cent by 1997 (and has fallen a good deal further since). Again with something of a lag, long-term unemployment has also now fallen very considerably.

Tax and social security policies can also be a key determinant of the welfare of families and children, and during the 1970s and 1980s these policies tended to disadvantage families with children. From a social welfare perspective, increases in social welfare pensions were seen as providing a way of targeting resources to a needy group without distorting financial incentives to work. As a result, at one point rates of payment for many of the unemployed were close to 40 per cent of average household income (adjusted for household size), while those on social insurance pensions received close to 60 per cent of that mean.

Since then, following the recommendations of the government-appointed Commission on Social Welfare, the rates of support for different contingencies have been brought much closer together, with what had been the lowest rates of support receiving above-average increases. On the tax side, erosion of the real value of allowances and bands pulled an ever-increasing proportion of the population into the tax net. From the mid-1980s no account was taken of the presence of children in determining the amount of tax paid by those in the tax net, as support was concentrated in the universal (and untaxed) Child Benefit, paid monthly in respect of all children. Tax exemption limits were however raised for those with children from the late 1980s, and the Family Income Supplement cash support for low-income working families has been expanded over time in terms of coverage and support rates.

From 1994 to 1997, social welfare support rates for the unemployed, the ill or disabled and pensioners rose by about 12 per cent on average. This was well ahead of prices, but not sufficient to keep up with average or median incomes from which relative income poverty lines are derived: mean (equivalised) household income rose by more than 20 per cent. The numbers relying on social welfare fell over the period due to falling unemployment, but as we shall see the relative income poverty rates of those who remained unemployed rose. This is in brief the background against which trends in child poverty described in Chapter 2 occurred, and we now seek to get behind those trends by looking at the types of household involved.

4.3. LABOUR FORCE PARTICIPATION

Focusing on the period 1980 to 1987, Callan *et al* (1989) showed that the dominant factor increasing income poverty rates for families with children was unemployment. A decomposition exercise distinguished the impact of changes in the distribution of families across (household head) labour force status categories and changes in poverty risk for those categories. This showed that almost all the pronounced increased risk in relative income poverty for families with children over that period was attribut-

able to changes in their distribution across labour force categories, and in particular the increase in numbers unemployed.

From 1987 to 1994, the percentage of households headed by
an unemployed person in our samples fell only marginally, from
10.6 per cent to 10.2 per cent, while the risk of being below half
average income increased slightly for such households. As a result, unemployment continued to be the dominant factor underlying income poverty for families with children. Over the 1994 to
1997 period, however, unemployment fell markedly and a rather
different pattern emerged. Table 4.1 shows that considerable
changes took place in the composition of the households below
the 50 per cent line over this period. We see that households
headed by an unemployed person accounted for a substantially
lower proportion of all those below the line by 1997, down from
one-third to just over one-fifth, because of the substantial decline
in the level of unemployment combined with a stable risk.
Households headed by an employee and by a retired person, on
the other hand, saw an increase in risk and as a result became
more important among those below the line.

*Table 4.1: Breakdown of Households Below 50% Relative Income
Poverty Line by Labour Force Status of Head, 1987, 1994 and 1997*

	1987	1994	1997
	%	%	%
Employee	8.2	6.5	12.7
Self-employed	4.8	5.8	7.7
Farmer	23.7	8.8	3.8
Unemployed	37.4	32.0	21.1
Ill/disabled	11.1	9.3	9.8
Retired	8.1	10.7	15.7
Home duties	6.7	27.0	28.9
All	100	100	100

*Equivalence scale 1/0.66/0.33.

So what was the impact of these changes on children? Table 4.2 takes children as the unit of analysis, and shows first their distribution across households in terms of the labour force status of the head in 1987, 1994 and 1997. This shows that in 1987 and 1994, 20 per cent of all children lived in households where the head was unemployed, but by 1997 this had fallen to 14 per cent. This was balanced by an increase in the percentage of children in households where the head is an employee. There was also a marked increase between 1987 and 1994 in the percentage of children living in households where the head works full-time in the home, which then stabilised to 1997 — most of these heads being female lone parents.

Table 4.2: Breakdown of Children by Labour Force Status of Household Head, and Poverty Risk with 50% Relative Income Poverty Line, 1987, 1994 and 1997

	% of all children			% of these falling below 50% line		
	1987	*1994*	*1997*	*1987*	*1994*	*1997*
Employee	51.2	48.8	53.3	5.8	6.3	8.7
Self-employed	10.7	11.3	11.4	13.7	18.4	19.4
Farmer	10.4	7.8	8.4	38.1	31.5	12.0
Unemployed	19.2	19.5	13.6	69.7	72.2	75.9
Ill/disabled	4.1	2.6	4.8	57.1	64.5	66.8
Retired	0.9	1.1	0.5	19.8	24.4	42.4
Home duties	3.4	8.8	8.0	34.6	66.1	55.4
All	**100.0**	**100**	**100**	**25.5**	**29.5**	**26.0**

The table then shows how the poverty risk for each of these household types changed over the period, using the 50 per cent relative income poverty line. We see that the risk associated with unemployment for the household head rose slightly: 76 per cent of children in households headed by an unemployed person were below half average income in 1997, com-

pared with 72 per cent in 1994. There was also a marginal increase for households where the head was an employee,
though for farmers there was a significant fall. There was also a
decline in risk for households with children where the head was
working full-time in the home, though their poverty rate was
still 55 per cent in 1997.

These changes in the size of the groups and their poverty
risks produced the changes in the composition of the low-
income households in which children live detailed in Table 4.3.
We see that in 1987 and 1994, about half of the children below
the 50 per cent relative income line lived in households headed
by an unemployed person. By 1997, this had fallen to 40 per
cent. The proportion in farm households also fell. This was balanced by an increase in the proportion in households headed
by an employee, or by an ill or disabled person.

*Table 4.3: Breakdown of Children in Households Below 50%
Relative Income Poverty Line by Labour Force Status of Household
Head, 1987, 1994 and 1997*

	1987	1994	1997
	%	%	%
Employee	11.6	10.4	17.7
Self-employed	5.7	7.1	8.5
Farmer	15.5	8.3	3.9
Unemployed	52.5	47.8	39.7
Ill/disabled	9.2	5.6	12.3
Retired	0.7	0.9	0.9
Home duties	4.7	19.8	17.0
All	**100**	**100**	**100**

*Equivalence scale 1/0.66/0.33

With these poverty risk and incidence figures, the fall in unemployment can be seen to be central to the overall fall in the

proportion of children living in households below half average income from 1994 to 1997. If the poverty risks facing each group had remained unchanged at their 1994 levels, then the changing distribution of children across these groups would itself have reduced the overall poverty rate for children with the 50 per cent line to about 26 per cent. This is because children were in effect moving from the group with the highest risk — where the head is unemployed — to the one with the lowest risk — where the head is an employee. Nonetheless, four out of every ten children below the 50 per cent line in 1997 were in households where the head was unemployed.

In total, about 70 per cent of the children below the 50 per cent line in 1997 were in households where the head was not in paid work. More strikingly, perhaps, fully two-thirds were in households receiving no income from work — no member of the household was receiving income from employment or self-employment. The observation was made at the end of Chapter 3 that one of the distinguishing features of Ireland's situation in comparative perspective was the extent to which households with children had no-one at work. In the 1997 LII survey, one in five Irish children lives in a household where no-one is in paid work. Thus the extent of inactivity, including not only unemployment but illness and disability and working outside the paid labour force, and the way in which inactivity is concentrated in certain households with children, is a key factor underlying child poverty.

Households where the head is working full-time in the home constitute a particularly interesting sub-group in that context, containing 17 per cent of all children below the 50 per cent line. In-depth examination of these households reveals that almost three-quarters of the household heads are never-married lone parents, while a further 20 per cent are separated or divorced. Very often there are two or more children, and in most cases the household head is aged over 30 — these are not predominantly young lone parents with just one child — and there are often other adults in the household. Most rely on social welfare as the main or only income coming into the household, and the relationship between the poverty threshold and the level of support offered by the social welfare system is critical to their poverty risk. Since half average equivalent income in the 1997 survey was about £80 per week, the 50 per cent relative income poverty line for an adult with two children (with the 1/0.66/0.33 equivalence scale) was about £130 per week. At the time the survey was carried out, the total cash payment from the social welfare system to a lone parent with two children (from One-Parent family payment and Child Benefit) would have been about £100 per week, well short of the poverty line. Since the payment for each extra child fell short of 0.33 of the adult rate, the gap between the poverty line and the payment widens as the number of children in the household increases.

While they contain less than one-fifth of all poor children, it is of interest to investigate why some households where the head is an employee fall below the 50 per cent line. Examination of these households reveals that in almost all cases the head is married, with spouse living in the household and working full-time in the home. In addition to the employee income of the head usually being the main income source, these are generally large households: three-quarters contain five or more people. About one in four have a disposable income of over £250 per week, but fall below the poverty threshold because of the number of people this has to support. About a half are on incomes of between £150 and £250, and a combination of this relatively low income and the size of the household is enough to leave them below the poverty threshold. Finally, about one-quarter have in fact little or no income from employment, and the reported income of the household is mostly from social welfare. This will usually arise when someone has just taken up a job and not been paid yet, but was on social welfare in the previous week.

Moving on to the 60 per cent relative income line, Table 4.4 shows that households headed by an employee become more important between 1994 and 1997. By the later year more than one-quarter of all children below this line were living in households headed by an employee, but the decline in unemployment is again central to the fall in the child poverty rate. Just as the dramatic rise in unemployment between 1980 and 1987 pushed many households with children into relative income poverty, the fall in unemployment between 1994 and 1997 has pulled many over these relative income lines.

Table 4.4: Poverty Risk Children by Labour Force Status of Household Head with 60% Relative Income Poverty Line, 1987, 1994 and 1997

	1987	1994	1997
	% below 60% Line		
Employee	16.5	13.7	18.5
Self-employed	22.1	24.8	30.2
Farmer	49.7	42.2	23.8
Unemployed	81.4	85.9	81.8
Ill/disabled	76.2	95.6	93.8
Retired	37.1	25.6	54.7
Home duties	78.7	89.9	75.2
All	**37.8**	**40.2**	**37.2**

Why then did the percentage of children falling below the lowest, 40 per cent, line rise between 1994 and 1997? This group has about the same proportion of household heads unemployed as those below the 50 per cent line; it has a higher proportion in households headed by a self-employed person, balanced by a lower proportion headed by an ill or disabled person.

However, Table 4.5 shows that the evolution of poverty risks for
the different labour force status groups was rather different with
this line. This risk increased sharply for households headed by
an unemployed person, those in home duties, and the retired
(although very few children are in the latter), as well as increasing for employees and the self-employed. For the first
three groups, the fact that the 40 per cent line more or less
"caught up" with some social welfare support rates over the
period is crucial. This can be seen more clearly when we also
take into account household size and composition, to which we
turn in the next section.

*Table 4.5: Poverty Risk for Children by Labour Force Status of
Household Head with 40% Relative Income Poverty Line, 1987,
1994 and 1997*

	1987	1994	1997
	% below 40% Line		
Employee	1.2	1.0	5.0
Self-employed	4.9	12.4	16.9
Farmer	22.5	12.4	3.9
Unemployed	14.5	20.0	39.9
Ill/disabled	20.0	18.3	19.6
Retired	6.1	6.2	35.9
Home duties	14.7	7.1	21.6
All	**7.6**	**7.6**	**13.2**

4.4 HOUSEHOLD SIZE AND COMPOSITION

We now turn to trends in risk and incidence distinguishing different types of household, in terms of size and composition, in
which children live in 1987, 1994 and 1997. Table 4.6 shows first
how children were distributed across the different types. We
see that there has been an increase over time in the percentage
of children living in households of two adults and one or two

children, and a sharp decline in the percentage living in households of two adults with four or more children — reflecting the decline in family size. There was also an increase between 1987 and 1994 in the proportion of children living with one adult, or with three or more adults. Recalling that the definition of child being employed is under 14 years of age, many of the latter are households containing older offspring as well as under-14s.

Table 4.6: Breakdown of Children by Household Type, and Poverty Risk with 50% Relative Income Poverty Line, 1987, 1994 and 1997

	1987	1994	1997	1987	1994	1997
	% of All Children			*% Falling below 50% Line**		
2 adults 1 child	5.9	6.6	9.9	16.6	14.2	16.2
2 adults 2 children	18.1	18.8	23.1	18.0	12.9	12.2
2 adults 3 children	19.9	18.6	20.4	21.2	22.0	31.4
2 adults 4+children	24.1	12.4	7.9	37.8	41.7	45.4
1 adult +children	2.8	6.2	5.4	31.7	56.4	44.4
3+ adults +child(ren)	29.2	37.4	33.3	24.2	35.6	26.7
All	**100.0**	**100**	**100**	**25.5**	**29.5**	**26.0**

*Equivalence scale 1/0.66/0.33

The table then shows the poverty risk for children in each of these household types, with the 50 per cent relative income line. This was consistently greatest for two adults with four or more children and for those living with only one adult across the three years. The most pronounced increase in risk over time was for children living with only one adult, where the poverty rate rose from under one-third in 1987 to over a half in 1994, before falling back to the still very high figure of 44 per cent in 1997.

In Table 4.7 one can see the type of household in which children below the 50 per cent relative income line lived, the product of the overall distribution across these household types and their poverty risk. We see that in 1987, about 36 per cent were in households comprising two adults and four or more children, while a further 28 per cent were in households comprising three or more adults with children. In 1994, the corresponding figures were 18 per cent and 46 per cent. By 1997, a considerably higher proportion of the children below the 50 per cent line were in households comprising two adults with one to three children. It is worth noting that, despite Ireland's increasing lone parenthood rate, only about one in ten of the children in households below the 50 per cent line were in single-adult households, and this did not increase between 1994 and 1997.

Table 4.7: Breakdown of Children in Households Below 50% Relative Income Poverty Line by Household Composition, Living in Ireland Surveys 1994 and 1997

	1987	1994	1997
	%	%	%
2 adults 1 child	3.8	3.2	6.2
2 adults 2 children	12.7	8.2	11.8
2 adults 3 children	16.5	13.8	24.3
2 adults 4+children	35.8	17.5	13.4
1 adult +children	3.5	11.8	9.0
3+ adults +child(ren)	27.7	45.5	35.3
All	**100.0**	**100**	**100**

*Equivalence scale 1/0.66/0.33

Children below the income poverty lines are in larger families on average than other children. Table 4.8 shows that children in households below the 60 per cent line in 1987 had an average family size (in terms of number of children aged under 14) of about 3.5, compared with 2.8 for those in households above that line. By 1997 the average number of children had fallen, both for those above and below the relative income lines, but the gap between them remained.

Table 4.8: Mean Family Size for Children in Households Below Relative Income Poverty Lines, 1987, 1994 and 1997

	1987	1994	1997
Children in Households	*Mean Number of Children in Family*		
Below 40% line	3.55	3.08	2.97
Below 50% line	3.56	3.07	2.77
Below 60% line	3.42	2.99	2.65
Above 60% line	2.78	2.42	2.15
All	**3.02**	**2.65**	**2.34**

*Equivalence scale 1/0.66/0.33

We investigate in Table 4.9 how this higher poverty risk for larger families comes about, by looking at the variation in risk across those with one or two children, three children, and four or more children, by the labour force status of the household head. We see that where the household head is at work, the risk is much greater for those with four or more children than for smaller families. Where the head is relying on social welfare, the pattern is less pronounced, though there is a striking difference between the risk for one-child households and larger ones where the head is in home duties.

Overall, this pattern of poverty risk and incidence highlights the importance of trends in the level of unemployment and in levels of social welfare support vis-à-vis other incomes. Between 1994 and 1997, falling unemployment pulled significant numbers of families with children above the 50 per cent and 60 per cent relative income lines. Because those continuing to be dependent on social welfare lagged behind average incomes, however, there was an increase in their poverty risk. In particular, the sharp rise in the percentage of children falling below the 40 per cent line reflects the fact that by 1997 the support for families provided by some social welfare programmes had fallen to at or about the 40 per cent line, having previously been for the most part above it. By 1997, the 40 per cent line for a couple with two children under 14 was £145 per week, exactly the rate then payable to such a family in short-term Unemployment Assistance (combined with Child Benefit). In addition, the equivalence scales being used here impute the "needs" of a full adult to all those aged 14 or over, including those aged 14-17, whereas the social welfare system continues to pay only the child dependant additions. As a result, the 40 per cent poverty line for a couple with two children aged 15 and 17 in 1997 was £187, but they would still only receive £145 in short-term UA. Close to half the children in households headed by an unemployed person and below the 40 per cent line in 1997 are thus in families falling into our category "three or more adults with children".

Table 4.9: Poverty Risk for Children in Different Family Sizes by Labour Force Status of Household Head with 50% Relative Income Poverty Line, 19987, 1997

	% below 50% Line		
	1-2 children	*3 children*	*4 or more children*
Employee	5.9	4.5	33.4
Self-employed	10.9	20.6	44.3
Farmer	19.4	0.8	9.6
Unemployed	65.6	81.0	82.4
Ill/disabled	72.7	40.9	86.6
Home duties	31.0	92.6	84.9
All	**17.7**	**30.8**	**51.8**

4.5 CONCLUSIONS

This chapter has shown that, just as rising unemployment produced increasing relative income poverty for Irish children in the 1980s, the fall in unemployment between 1994 and 1997 was central to the decline in the proportion of children living in households below half or 60 per cent of average income. In 1994, 20 per cent of all children lived in households where the head was unemployed, but by 1997 this had fallen to 14 per cent. The relative income poverty risk associated with unemployment rose from 1994 to 1997, however, as social welfare support levels lagged behind rapidly-increasing average incomes. This contributed to the divergent pattern with the lowest relative income line, where the poverty risk for children actually rose, reflecting the fact that this line had in effect caught up with social welfare support rates. Across all the relative income poverty lines risk also increased for households where the head was an employee or self-employed, as some of those in work failed to keep up with the rapid increase in average incomes. Children living in larger families continued to be at high risk of relative income poverty, even where the head was in work. Where the household was relying on social welfare, the poverty risk for such children was very high indeed.

Chapter 5

Poverty and Deprivation

5.1 INTRODUCTION

So far we have focused on household incomes, but we now wish to broaden that focus. Poverty is conventionally defined in terms of exclusion due to lack of resources, but low income on its own may not be an entirely satisfactory measure of such exclusion. In this chapter we therefore combine income with non-monetary indicators of deprivation, to assess how the position of families with children has evolved. In Section 5.2 we outline the rationale and general approach to be taken. Section 5.3 presents the trends in child poverty using poverty measures incorporating both income and non-monetary indicators. Section 5.4 looks at the composition of the groups identified as poor using this approach versus income lines alone, while Section 5.5 summarises the conclusions.

5.2. USING NON-MONETARY INDICATORS IN MEASURING CHILD POVERTY

Low income alone may not be reliable as an indicator of poverty, because it often fails to distinguish households experiencing deprivation and exclusion. This is not primarily because of the (real) difficulties in measuring income accurately, but more because a household's command over resources is affected by much more than its current income. Long-term factors, relating most importantly to the way resources have been accumulated or eroded over time, as well as current income play a crucial role in influencing the likelihood of current deprivation and exclusion.

Two complementary routes can be pursued in moving away from reliance on income at a particular point in time. The first is to measure income as it evolves over time by means of longitudinal surveys. The second is to measure various aspects of living standards and deprivation directly through non-monetary indicators. The use of such indicators was pioneered by Townsend (1979), and they have been used in studying poverty from a cross-section perspective in for example Mack and Lansley (1985), Mayer and Jencks (1988), Mayer (1993), Muffels (1993), Callan, Nolan and Whelan (1993), Hallerod (1995) and Nolan and Whelan (1996). These studies have sought to use non-monetary indicators in rather different ways. They all face hard questions-such as how the most satisfactory indicators for the purpose are to be selected, whether they are to be combined into a summary deprivation measure and if so how, and how they are then to be employed in exploring poverty.

It may be particularly important to know the extent to which distinct dimensions of deprivation can be identified, since some may be better than others as measures of generalised deprivation and exclusion. In earlier research with data from the 1987 ESRI survey, three such dimensions were identified (Nolan and Whelan, 1996):

1. *Basic life-style deprivation* — enforced absence of basic items such as food or clothing, considered by most people to be necessities;

2. *Secondary life-style deprivation* — enforced absence of items such as cars, telephone and holidays commonly possessed but not considered by a majority of people to be necessities.

3. *Housing deprivation* — enforced absence of items relating to housing such as having an indoor toilet, hot and cold running water, or a bath/shower, generally considered to be necessities but absence of which bore a weak relationship to other types of deprivation.

In seeking to identify those excluded due to a lack of resources, we have concentrated on the basic deprivation index. These items clearly represented socially perceived necessities: they were possessed by most people, they reflect rather basic aspects of current material deprivation, and they cluster together, which lends support to the notion that they are useful as indicators of the underlying generalised deprivation we are trying to measure. Focusing on households that are both at relatively low income levels and experiencing basic deprivation should then give a better indication of the scale of generalised deprivation or exclusion due to lack of resources than those below income lines alone. This way of identifying those most in need has been incorporated in the global poverty reduction target adopted in the National Anti-Poverty Strategy, which forms the benchmark against which progress in combating poverty is assessed (NAPS 1997). A detailed discussion of aggregate trends between 1994 and 1997, against which the pattern for children can be set, is given in Callan *et al* (1999).

5.3 TRENDS IN CHILD POVERTY

Table 5.1 shows for 1987, 1994 and 1997 the percentage of households falling below 40, 50 and 60 per cent of mean equivalent income (using equivalence scale 1/0.66/0.33) *and* experiencing enforced basic deprivation.[1] Between 1987 and 1994 there was little change in the extent of poverty overall

---

[1] The deprivation indicators are not available in the 1973 and 1980 CSO surveys.

shown by these combined income and deprivation measures. Between 1994 and 1997, by contrast, there has been a marked fall in the percentage below the relative income lines and experiencing basic deprivation with the highest, 60 per cent, income line. The percentage below that line and experiencing basic deprivation has fallen from 15 per cent to 10 per cent. The percentage below the 50 per cent relative income line and experiencing basic deprivation has also fallen, though less sharply, while the percentage below the 40 per cent line and experiencing such deprivation has risen slightly. Thus, combining relative income poverty lines with a deprivation criterion held fixed from 1987 to 1997 gives a very different picture for all households to that described with the relative income lines alone.

Table 5.1: Percentage of Households and Persons Below Relative Income Thresholds and Experiencing Basic Deprivation, 1987, 1994 and 1997

Relative Income Line	% of Households below Line and Experiencing Enforced Basic Deprivation		
	1987	*1994*	*1997*
% of Households			
40% line	3.3	2.3	3.0
50% line	9.8	9.1	7.3
60% line	16.0	14.8	9.9
% of persons			
40% line	3.7	3.4	4.6
50% line	12.2	11.2	8.5
60% line	17.7	17.0	11.0

* Equivalence scale 1/0.66/0.33

Turning to persons, the table also shows the percentage of persons in households meeting these relative income plus deprivation criteria in each year. We see first that the percentage of persons is greater than the corresponding percentage of households in each case: "poor" households are larger than average. Secondly, though, the trend between 1994 and 1997 was very much the same for persons as for households: an increase in the numbers below the 40 per cent line and experiencing basic deprivation, but a fall in the numbers below each of the other income lines and experiencing such deprivation.

What about children? The available indicators were designed to measure the extent and nature of deprivation at the level of the household rather than the individual. As in using household income to measure poverty, the assumption is made that pooling resources within the household equalises living standards and poverty risk for all household members. The situation where children are in poverty because of insufficient sharing of resources within the household will not be captured, either with conventional income measures or with the deprivation indicators we have available here. (Some indicators specifically designed to capture deprivation among children are, however, being included in the 1999 wave of the Living in Ireland Survey, as we discuss in Chapter 6.) On that basis, we can see what these indicators, together with income, tell us about the households in which children live.

Table 5.2 shows the percentage of children and adults in households below the relative income lines and experiencing basic deprivation in 1987, 1994 and 1997. We see first that the poverty rates on this basis for children are a good deal higher than the corresponding rates for adults. For example, 15 per cent of all adults but 24 per cent of all children were in households below the 60 per cent relative income line and experiencing basic deprivation in 1994. These are rather wider gaps between children and adults than that those shown by the relative income lines in that year, discussed in Section 5.

Table 5.2: Percentage of Children and Adults in Households Below Relative Income Thresholds and Experiencing Basic Deprivation, 1987, 1994 and 1997

Relative Income Line	% of Households below Line and Experiencing Enforced Basic Deprivation		
	1987	*1994*	*1997*
% of children			
40% line	4.6	4.1	8.6
50% line	18.5	17.9	14.9
60% line	24.8	23.5	16.9
% of adults			
40% line	3.4	3.2	3.6
50% line	9.5	9.0	6.8
60% line	14.6	14.8	9.4

* Equivalence scale 1/0.66/0.33

In terms of trends over the 1994–97 period, we see that the percentage of children in households below the 40 per cent income line and experiencing basic deprivation rose sharply between 1994 and 1997, but that with the 50 per cent and especially the 60 per cent income line the percentage fell. This is similar to the direction of change shown for children by the corresponding income lines alone, though the scale of the fall is much greater when we look at the numbers below the 60 per cent line and experiencing basic deprivation than just those below that income line.

It is worth noting that for adults, on the other hand, there is a marked contrast between trends with the income lines alone and those with the income plus deprivation measures. For adults, we see that the percentage falling below the 50 per cent and 60 per cent income lines and experiencing basic deprivation fell by at least as much as for children between 1994 and 1997, despite the fact that as we saw earlier their income poverty rates rose. This pronounced fall in deprivation, at a time when relative income poverty was rising, is attributable to the very rapid rates of income growth experienced over the period. As explored in detail in Callan *et al* (1999), the contrast brings out that in such a period of rapid growth, relative income lines on their own may miss out on an important part of the story. The official global poverty reduction target adopted in 1997 by the Irish government's National Anti-Poverty Strategy focuses on the numbers falling below 50 per cent or 60 per cent of mean income and experiencing basic deprivation. As a result of the declines in this measures now shown by the 1997 data, this target has recently been rebased to aim at a greater fall than initially envisaged (see NAPS 1999). Had the target been framed simply in terms of relative income poverty, on the other hand, the 1997 data would have suggested that poverty got worse over the period.

Here is not the place to explore the best way to frame such targets — we argue in Callan *et al* (1999) for a tiered set of targets encompassing real income levels, deprivation indicators that adjust over time to enhanced expectations, and relative income levels. The point of most relevance here is that in terms of the (50 per cent or 60 per cent) relative income lines combined with basic deprivation measures, the position of children improved between 1994 and 1997, but the pronounced gap between them and adults did not narrow in the same way as the gap in relative income poverty rates.

5.4 RISK AND INCIDENCE

We have seen that the combined income and deprivation poverty measures show a rather different pattern over time to relative income poverty lines alone. It is clearly important then from a targeting perspective to know whether these poverty measures identify the same types of households with children as poor as do the relative income poverty lines. Table 5.3 compares the

children in households below half average income with those
falling below the higher 60 per cent line but also experiencing
basic deprivation, in 1987, 1994 and 1997, in terms of the labour
force status of the head of the household in which they live. We
see that self-employment (including farming) is consistently
less important for those below the higher income line and experiencing basic deprivation than for those below the half average income line. In 1994 and even more so in 1997, unemployment is rather more prominent with the combined low income plus deprivation criterion: more than half the children in
households below the 60 per cent income line and experiencing basic deprivation are in households headed by an unemployed person. Strikingly, none are in households headed by a
farmer. About 16 per cent of "poor" children by the combined
income plus deprivation criterion are in households headed by
an employee. Looking in more depth at this sub-group, we find
that in most cases there are five or more persons in the household combined with low income from work, rather than simply
very low earnings. About the same number are in households
headed by someone working full-time in the home, and these
households are relying for the most part on social welfare
transfers. In most cases the household head is aged over thirty
rather than a young lone parent, there are generally at least two
adults in the household rather than only one, and almost all
these households are below not only the 60 per cent line but
also half average income.

This profile of children in poor households reflects the pattern of poverty risk by labour force status shown in Table 5.4.
We see that fully two-thirds of the children in households
headed by an unemployed person in 1997 were below the 60
per cent income line and experiencing basic deprivation. The
other groups facing high poverty risks, though lower than that,
were children in households headed by someone who was ill or
disabled, or working full-time in the home.

Table 5.3: Breakdown of Children in "Poor" Households by Labour Force Status of Household Head, ESRI Surveys 1987, 1994 and 1997

	Below 50% line	Below 60% plus deprivation	Below 50% line	Below 60% plus deprivation	Below 50% line	Below 60% plus deprivation
	1987		1994		1997	
	%	%	%	%	%	%
Employee	11.6	17.9	10.4	12.0	17.7	16.1
Self-employed	5.7	3.2	7.1	1.7	8.5	4.0
Farmer	15.5	8.6	8.3	3.2	3.9	0
Unemployed	52.5	51.5	47.8	52.0	39.7	53.2
Ill/disabled	9.2	10.7	5.6	5.8	12.3	10.4
Retired	0.7	.8	0.9	0.7	0.9	0.6
Home duties	4.7	7.3	19.8	24.7	17.0	15.8
All	100	100	100	100	100	100
% of all children	25.5	24.8	29.6	23.5	26.0	16.9

*Equivalence scale 1/0.66/0.33

Table 5.4: Poverty Risk for Children by Labour Force Status of Household Head with 60% Relative Income Line Plus Basic Deprivation, 1997

	% below 60% Line and Experiencing Basic Deprivation
Employee	5.1
Self-employed	5.0
Farmer	0
Unemployed	66.6
Ill/disabled	43.3
Retired	17.3
Home duties	36.3

Turning to household composition, Table 5.5 shows the pattern of poverty risk and incidence for children in households of different types in 1997 using the combined income and deprivation criteria. Poverty risk is consistently high for children in larger households, being particularly low for couples with one or two children. Only 4 per cent of all poor children by this measure are in households comprising one adult with children, though 44 per cent are in households of three or more adults with children.

Table 5.5: Poverty Risk and Incidence for Children by Household Type with 60% Relative Income Line Plus Basic Deprivation, 1997

	% below 60% Line and Experiencing Basic Deprivation	% of Children below 60% Line and Experiencing Basic Deprivation
2 adults 1 child	4.2	2.4
2 adults 2 children	6.5	8.5
2 adults 3 children	23.3	28.5
2 adults 4+children	29.0	13.3
1 adult +children	13.7	3.6
3+ adults +child(ren)	23.1	43.6

5.5 CONCLUSIONS

Low income on its own may not be an entirely satisfactory measure of exclusion due to lack of resources. In this chapter we therefore combined income with non-monetary indicators of deprivation, to assess how the position of families with children has evolved. Using poverty measures combining 50 per cent or 60 per cent relative income lines with basic deprivation, the position of children was seen to have improved between 1994 and 1997. However, the pronounced gap between children and adults did not narrow with these measures in the same way as the gap in their relative income poverty rates. As a result, in 1997 about 17 per cent of children were in households both below 60 per cent of mean equivalised income and experiencing basic deprivation, compared with about 9 per cent of adults.

Compared with children below the relative income lines alone, a smaller proportion of the children meeting the combined income and deprivation poverty criteria in 1997 were in households headed by a self-employed person or farmer and more were in households where the head was unemployed. Indeed, more than half the children in households below the 60 per cent relative income line and experiencing basic deprivation were in households headed by an unemployed person. Unemployment has continued falling since 1997, and we return in the final chapter to the likely impact of continued economic growth since then on the scale and nature of child poverty. First, in Chapter 6 we switch from the cross-sectional perspective to begin exploring the dynamics of income and income poverty for Irish children from one year to the next.

Chapter 6

Child Poverty and Income/Deprivation Dynamics

6.1 INTRODUCTION

We have seen in previous chapters that research on poverty, including child poverty, generally focuses on income at a point in time, and that non-monetary deprivation indicators can play a valuable role in complementing such income measures. One reason why current income does not tell us all we need to know about a household's living standards is that it changes over time, and income in the longer-term — what economists call "permanent income" — also exerts a major influence on living standards. This also provides the rationale for directly exploring the dynamics of income and of child income poverty.

This involves measuring the income of a specific set of households with children at various points in time, via different waves of a longitudinal household survey. One can then see how much movement there is in and out of income poverty. We begin such an analysis here for Irish children, drawing on material prepared as part of a UNICEF project on the dynamics of child poverty in industrialised countries.[1] We also use non-

[1] The analysis summarised here benefited from very helpful comments and advice from Bruce Bradbury, Markus Janti, Stephen Jenkins, John Micklewright and participants in a workshop at ICDC Florence, October 1998.

monetary indicators of deprivation, of the type employed in
Chapter 5, to help in assessing the implications of income poverty dynamics for living standards.

6.2 CHILD INCOME POVERTY DYNAMICS

The data set on which we rely was gathered in the first two
waves of the Living in Ireland Survey for the European Community Household Panel (ECHP). Wave 1 was carried out in the
second half of 1994, Wave 2 in the same period in 1995. We
have already seen in Chapter 2 that the achieved sample size in
1994 was 4,048 households. In the second wave, 3,430 of these
plus 154 "generated" households were successfully inter-
viewed.[2] The survey obtained *inter alia* detailed data on income
from various sources accruing to each household member in
the previous calendar year, and it is this income concept — the
one also employed by Eurostat in the comparative ECHP-based
figures presented in Chapter 3 — on which we focus here. It
differs from the income measure used in our main analyses of
poverty trends in Chapters 3 and 4, which refers for the most
part to income in the current week or month. Because Eurostat
has already constructed annual income for the first two waves,
income dynamics can now be studied using that measure. Income is now equivalised using the square root of household
size, the scale employed in the UNICEF project, and children
are taken to be all those aged under 18.

The pattern of income dynamics for Irish children from Wave
1 to Wave 2 has been measured by attributing to each child the
equivalised income of their household. The extent of mobility

---

[2] The following rule is that in principle all members of the household in Wave
1 are followed in the second and subsequent waves, whether the household
has "split" or not and whether such splits are due to divorce or any other factor. Those who turn out to have emigrated or moved into a non-household
institution are not, however, retained within the panel. In practice, some types
of split may of course make follow-up more difficult than others.

has been measured in terms of the income categories below 40 per cent of the median, between 40-50 per cent of the median, between 50-60 per cent of the median, or above 60 per cent of the median. Table 6.1 shows the location in Wave 2 of children categorised by their income in Wave 1.

Table 6.1: Children by Household Income in Wave 1 and Wave 2, Ireland 1994–95

	Income in Wave 2 as % of median				
Income in Wave 1 as % of median	*y<40%*	*40% <= y <50%*	*50% <= y <60%*	*60% <= y*	*All*
Y<40%	46	12	4	37	100
40% <= y <50%	5	52	27	17	100
50% <= y <60%	4	15	42	39	100
60% <= y	3	3	5	89	100
All	5	10	12	73	100

One of the most striking findings is the extent of mobility for those on very low incomes in Wave 1. The table shows that 46 per cent of those below 40 per cent of the median in Wave 1 were still in that position in Wave 2. However, fully 37 per cent of that group had seen their household incomes rise to over 60 per cent of the median by Wave 2. By contrast, of those between 40 per cent and 50 per cent of the median in Wave 1, only 17 per cent had risen to above 60 per cent by Wave 2. So the group on very low incomes includes a disproportionate number experiencing relatively substantial income increases. This is consistent with the notion that very low income in a cross-section may not always be a good indicator of permanent income, as reflected in the relatively low average deprivation scores for this group. The pattern of income dynamics also serves to reveal, though, that a substantial sub-set do stay on very low incomes for at least two waves.

6.3. INCOME DYNAMICS AND DEPRIVATION LEVELS

A dynamic perspective on income can help us to understand the way in which deprivation levels vary across children's households. To explore this we also employ non-monetary indicators obtained in the European Community Household Panel survey. The ECHP contains information on the set of 17 non-monetary indicators, similar to those analysed in Chapter 5. While it was important to break these up into different clusters in Chapter 5, in distinguishing different dimensions and identifying generalised deprivation at a point in time, here we are focusing simply on the overall direction of change in deprivation levels over time. For simplicity, we therefore construct a single 17-item deprivation index. Unfortunately, differences in timing between the income and deprivation measures limit their value at this stage. The ECHP income measures from Wave 1 and Wave 2 relate to calendar years 1993 and 1994 respectively, but the deprivation information relates to the date of interview in late 1994 and late 1995 respectively. Deprivation as measured in each wave thus relates to a point 6-9 months after the end of year to which the income refers. While we cannot therefore relate changes in deprivation to changes in income, we can examine the deprivation scores of those on persistently low or high income versus those moving in or out of income poverty.

Table 6.2 first shows deprivation scores on the 17-item index in Wave 1, for children categorised by income poverty status in each wave. We see that children in poverty in both 1993 and in 1994 had an average deprivation score of 5.5. Those below the relative income line in Wave 1 but not Wave 2 had a significantly lower score of 4.8, not very different to those in poverty in Wave 2 but not Wave 1 who had a mean score of 4.6. Those above the income poverty line in both waves had the much lower average deprivation score of 3.0. So there is an extremely pronounced difference between those who were income poor in both versus neither waves, but there is also a marked difference between either of these and the intermediate group who were income poor in one but not the other wave.

Table 6.2: Deprivation Scores for Irish Children with 17-Item Deprivation Index, by Income Poverty Status in Each Wave (%)

	Poor in Both Waves	Poor in Wave 1 not Wave 2	Poor in Wave 2 not Wave 1	Poor in Neither Wave
Mean deprivation score in Wave 1	5.5	4.8	4.6	3.0
Mean deprivation score in Wave 2	5.4	4.5	4.2	2.4

Indeed, it is striking that very much the same pattern is seen when we focus on deprivation scores in Wave 2. The table also shows that, even though we are then looking at deprivation levels 6-9 months after the end of 1994, knowing poverty status in both 1993 and 1994 helps to predict deprivation levels. Those who were income poor in both 1993 and 1994 turn out to have much higher deprivation scores in mid-late 1995 than those who were poor in only one of those years, and very much higher than those who were poor in neither. Incomes in 1993 and 1994 do nearly as good a job in capturing the divergence in deprivation scores in 1995 as in 1994: again, testimony to the role of income over a prolonged period in influencing current deprivation levels.

6.4. DEPRIVATION DYNAMICS FOR IRISH CHILDREN

As well as income dynamics, we can also look at how deprivation scores themselves changed from Wave 1 to Wave 2: how many children were in households which experienced a decline in deprivation, and how many saw an increase? Table 6.3 shows the transition matrix for children in terms of their house-

hold's deprivation score in Waves 1 and 2, grouping deprivation scores into five categories which are similar in size.

This shows that 42 per cent of children were in households in
the same deprivation category in each wave. About 22 per cent
were in a higher category in Wave 2 than Wave 1, in other
words experiencing more deprivation. A greater number,
about 35 per cent, were less deprived in Wave 2 — reflecting
the overall decline in the mean level of deprivation.

*Table 6.3: Children by 17-item Deprivation Score in Wave 1 and
Wave 2, Ireland 1994-1995 (%)*

Deprivation Score in Wave 1	Deprivation Score in Wave 2					
	0	*1*	*2-3*	*4-5*	*6 +*	*All*
0	9.0	5.1	2.3	0.4	0.2	17.1
1	6.5	8.0	4.6	1.4	0.2	20.6
2-3	3.9	6.1	10.4	3.6	1.2	25.1
4-5	0.7	2.2	6.1	5.3	3.4	17.7
6 or more	0.3	0.7	3.3	5.4	9.8	19.5
All	**20.4**	**22.1**	**26.7**	**16.1**	**14.7**	**100**

For those with a score of zero in Wave 1, over half had the same
score in Wave 2. Similarly for those at the other extreme, with
score in Wave 1 of six or more, half remained at this relatively
high level of deprivation in Wave 2. The percentage with score
unchanged from Wave 1 to Wave 2 was somewhat less — about
30-40 per cent — at intermediate levels of deprivation. This reflects a common pattern whereby measured mobility is least in
the top and bottom categories because in effect movement can
only occur in one direction.

About 10 per cent of Irish children were in households which
had persistently high deprivation levels — scores of 6 or more
on the 17-item index — in the two waves of the ECHP. We saw
in the previous section that about the same number were in

households below the half median income poverty line in 1993 and 1994. There is a very substantial overlap between these two groups: about 85 per cent of those with very high deprivation scores were also below the income poverty line, and this figure would probably be slightly higher if one had exactly contemporaneous information on these two measures of welfare. Between them they must contain a very high proportion of the children most vulnerable to poverty. The differences in timing between the income and deprivation measures in the ECHP, already outlined, mean that we cannot at this stage analyse exactly how deprivation changes as income changes, but that will be possible in the near future.

6.5. CONCLUSIONS

We know from previous chapters that cross-section income measures alone will not tell us all we need to know about which children are in poverty. For example, some of those living in households on *very* low incomes at a particular point are not amongst those facing the greatest deprivation. From a policy perspective, the children most in need at a point in time, at whom social protection and other interventions should be targeted, are mostly to be found just below or just above an income poverty line such as half median income, rather than well below it. However, sustained low income, as indicated by careful analysis of longitudinal data on income dynamics, is more likely to be a good indicator of need. Even at this early stage, our findings suggest that information on both income dynamics and non-monetary indicators of household welfare and deprivation levels can substantially complement one another in helping policy-makers to identify and target poor children.

As further waves of the European Community Household Panel become available, or the full Irish data for 1995 and 1996 are brought into use, it will be possible using longitudinal data to directly link income and deprivation dynamics, in a way which we have not been able to do here. As we discuss in the next chapter, a key priority in terms of monitoring and tackling child poverty also has to be the incorporation of measures of deprivation relating directly to children themselves into the data sets which serve as the basis for analysis and poverty formulation.

Chapter 7

Measuring Child Well-being

7.1 INTRODUCTION

We have emphasised at various points the importance of going beyond current household income in measuring child poverty, in Chapter 5 in bringing out the value of non-monetary indicators of deprivation, and in Chapter 6 in looking at income dynamics together with these indicators. However, the indicators in question were designed to measure the extent and nature of deprivation at the level of the household, and tell us about the living standards of households containing children: they do not serve as direct measures of living standards or deprivation for the children themselves. The assumption is made that pooling resources within the household equalises living standards and poverty risk for all household members. The situation where children are in poverty because of insufficient sharing of resources within the household will not be captured, either with conventional income measures or with the deprivation indicators we have available.

Poverty research has found it very difficult to look within the household "black box", as brought out in, for example, Jenkins (1991). Non-monetary deprivation indicators do indeed have some potential for capturing differences in individual living standards within the household, as explored in Cantillon and Nolan (1998), and specially-designed indicators for children would be enormously valuable. We have developed a limited set of such indicators for inclusion in the 1999 wave of the Living in Ireland survey, and these are discussed in Section 7.2. Issues relating more broadly to the measurement and monitoring of child well being are discussed in Section 7.3.

7.2. DEVELOPING INDIVIDUAL-LEVEL DEPRIVATION INDICATORS

The indicators of deprivation generally included in large-scale household surveys are designed to measure the extent and nature of deprivation at the level of the household. The potential of indicators designed to measure living standards at the level of the individual, but which can fit within the framework of traditional poverty research using large samples, has not yet received much attention in the research literature. Such indicators could allow differences between spouses, between young adults, their parents and the elderly in multi-family households, and between children and adults, to be measured.

The non-monetary deprivation indicators included in the 1987 ESRI household survey did have some potential for detecting differences in individual living standards between adults within the household, as brought out in Cantillon and Nolan (1998). The same survey actually also included four non-monetary indicators relating specifically to children. These were analysed in Nolan and Farrell's (1990) study of child poverty, and related to being unable to afford:

- Toys or leisure equipment for children,

- Separate bedrooms for different sexes for children over 10 years of age,

- Three meals a day for the children, and

- Education up to age 20 for all children.

Only a very small proportion of respondents in the survey said they could not afford three meals a day for the children — 1 per cent of all those with children, 3 per cent of those with children and below the 60 per cent relative income poverty line. A significantly higher proportion, about 6 per cent of all those with children and 9 per cent of those below the 60 per cent income line, said they could not afford separate bedrooms. The corresponding figures for not being able to afford toys were higher, at 7 per cent and 13 per cent respectively. Finally, about 17 per cent of all those with children, 23 per cent of those below the 60 per cent relative income line, said they could not afford education up to age 20 for all children.

In order to probe intra-household issues in greater depth, in the course of a separate project currently being carried out for the Combat Poverty Agency on that topic, a more extensive set of indicators has been developed and included in the 1999 Living in Ireland Survey. These focus for the most part on the living standards and control over resources of different adults within the household (see Cantillon and Nolan, 2000 for a description). However, where there are children (aged under 14) in the household, the mother is also asked the following:

"Over the last year, has lack of money meant that the children have had to do without:

a. A party on their birthday with friends

b. School trips

c. Having friends home to play

d. Doing lessons in, for example, music or dancing, or playing sports

e. Three meals a day

f. Pocket money

g. Toys such as dolls or models

h. A bicycle or sports equipment."

It is hoped that these indicators will allow a concrete picture of the types of deprivation facing children in poor households to be presented. They should also permit exploration of the extent to which an unequal distribution of resources within households contributes to deprivation for children.

7.3. MEASURING CHILD WELL-BEING

This study has concentrated on poverty and deprivation for Irish children, which can be seen as key indicators of the broader concept of child well-being. It would be enormously valuable to be able to place poverty and deprivation levels in their broader setting, by also presenting a battery of other indicators relating to other aspects of children's well-being and how these have been changing over time. To be able to do so, a coherent set of indicators on which information is available at regular intervals is required. The ground-work required in this area is considerable, but a beginning has been made in the review of the literature on children's well-being recently completed for the Combat Poverty Agency by Costello (1999) and there is also a great deal to be learned from recent developments elsewhere.

Perhaps the most notable recent innovation in this context has been the development of a limited but broad set of official indicators of child well-being in the USA, on which an annual monitoring report produced by the Federal Government is now based. The process of developing this set of indicators began with an intensive examination of the data actually available on a regular basis across the areas of health, education, economic security, the family and neighbourhood, and child development (see Hauser, Brown and Prosser , eds. 1997). In 1997, the federal government (through the Bureau of Labor Statistics and the Federal Interagency Forum on Child and Family Statistics) produced the first in what has become an annual series, *America's Children: Key Indicators of Well-Being*. In the report for 1999 issued recently, a set of core indicators are covered and trends over the past two decades are examined.

It is worth setting out the indicators involved, in order to illustrate concretely what is involved in the US case, and these are shown in Table 7.1. The central criterion is availability of regular, consistent, up-to-date information, and the central focus is on directions of change rather than levels.

Table 7.1: US Key National Indicators of Children's Well-being

Indicator	Description
Economic Security	
Child poverty and family income	Percentage of children in poverty
Secure parental employment	Percentage of children with at least one parent employed full-time all year
Housing problems	Percentage of households with children reporting specified housing problems
Food security	Percentage of children in households experiencing food insecurity
	Percentage of children aged 2–5 with a good diet
Access to health care	Percentage of children covered by health insurance
	Percentage of children with no usual source of health care
Health	
General health status	Percentage of children in very good or excellent health
Activity limitation	Percentage of children 5 or over with any limitation in activity from a chronic condition
Low birthweight	Percentage of infants weighing less than 5.5 pounds at birth
Infant mortality	Deaths before first birthday per 1,000 live births
Childhood immunizations	Percentage of children 19–35 months who received combined immunization

Child mortality	Deaths per 100,000 children aged 1–4
	Deaths per 100,000 children aged 5–14
Adolescent mortality	Deaths per 100,000 adolescents aged 15–19
Adolescent births	Births per 1,000 females aged 15-19
Behavioural and Social Environment	
Regular cigarette smoking	Percentage of 8th, 10th and 12th grade students who reported smoking daily
Alcohol use	Percentage of 8th, 10th and 12th grade students who reported having five or more alcoholic beverages in a row in the last 2 weeks
Illicit drug use	Percentage of 8th, 10th and 12th grade students who have used illicit drugs in the previous 30 days
Youth victims and perpetrators of violent crimes	Rate of serious violent crime victimization per 1,000 youths aged 12–17
	Serious violent crime offending rate per 1,000 youth aged 12–17
Education	
Family reading to young children	Percentage of children aged 3–5 who are read to every day by a family member
Early childhood education	Percentage of children aged 3–4 who are enrolled in preschool
Maths and reading achievement	Average maths scale (0-500) score of 9, 13 and 17-year-olds
	Average reading scale (0-500) score of 9, 13 and 17-year-olds
High school completion	Percentage of 18–24 year olds who have completed high school
Youth neither enrolled in school or working	Percentage of 16–19 year olds who are neither in school or working
Higher education	Percentage of high school graduates aged 25–29 who have completed a university degree

The indicators are grouped into four broad dimensions. Income poverty (using the official US poverty line) is a key indicator of economic security and other indicators of this aspect of child well-being are also used, but the more fundamental broadening out is the coverage of health, education, behaviour and social environment. This range of indicators provides a much more comprehensive, complex and varied picture of recent developments in child well-being than a single measure of child poverty. It shows for example that while the percentage of children in poverty in the USA was little changed from 1996 to 1997, many of the indicators of child health showed an improvement. The limitations of the available indicators are clearly acknowledged, and one important function of the publication is to highlight gaps in the available information.

Another example of recent efforts to monitor trends in child well-being, this time in a comparative context, is the study for UNICEF by Micklewright and Stewart (1999) of child welfare in the European Union. They use the following indicators:

Economic well-being

- GDP per capita
- Percentage of children in households below 50 per cent of national median income
- Prevalence of worklessness among households with children
- Unemployment for young adults.

Mortality

- Under-5 and young persons' mortality
- Death rate for 5–14-year-olds from road accidents
- Suicide rate for 15–24-year-old men.

Education

- Percentage of 16-year-olds in education
- Expenditure on education as per cent of GDP, adjusted for age structure.

Teenage Fertility

- Birth rate to 15–19-year-olds.

Life Satisfaction

- Percentage of 15–19-year-olds who classify themselves as satisfied with life.

On the basis of these indicators, they find rather mixed results when assessing the extent to which child welfare levels have converged over time among the member states. They emphasise the limitations of the indicators they have been able to cover, and the need both to analyse existing data from a children's perspective, but also to develop new, regular sources of statistics at European level.

Recent studies of child welfare and poverty in the UK have also pointed to the value of a range of indicators and employed specific ones to demonstrate the point. For example, a study for the Rowntree Foundation (Howarth *et al,* 1998) looked at the percentage of children living in households below half average income, the percentage in households with no-one at work, the low birthweight rate, the number of accidental child deaths, the percentage gaining no GCSE grade C or above, the number permanently excluded from school, the percentage of children whose parents divorce, the number of births to girls under age 16, and the numbers in young offenders' institutions. A slightly broader range has been employed by the OECD, whereas the World Bank and the UN — with a primary focus on developing countries — prioritise basic measures of infant and child mortality and school enrollment. Indicators like these have to be brought together from a variety of administrative and survey sources. Focuses on what can be covered in a single survey, the recent UK Millennium Survey on Poverty and Social Exclusion contains a particularly extensive set of non-monetary indicators of deprivation.

A review of the literature on children's well-being commissioned by the Combat Poverty Agency (Costello, 1999) also serves to bring out the range of areas and indicators of well-being one would wish to be able to monitor. The indicators it mentions include for example smoking during pregnancy, birthweight, early education, income adequacy, presence of good role models, access to leisure activities, and various aspects of schooling. A separate review of secondary data sources in relation to poverty, also commissioned by the Agency, should also help to point up areas where secondary data are available and could be used more effectively, as well as highlighting gaps in the information available on a regular basis. One very major gap in the Irish case is the fact that there is no national survey following the development of a cohort of children from birth, tracking the development and well-being of a representative sample over time. Such cohort studies have been highly influential in other countries, particularly in bringing out the complex interactions between different factors that can adversely affect children's development. The Commission on the Family among others has recommended that a longitudinal survey of a child birth cohort be initiated in Ireland, and this is now being actively considered. Monitoring the well-being of Irish children will also presumably be among the issues addressed by the National Children's Strategy, which is currently at the consultation stage and to which we return in the next chapter.

7.4 CONCLUSIONS

While the present study has concentrated on child poverty and deprivation, it would be enormously valuable to place this in its broader setting, drawing on a battery of indicators relating to other aspects of children's well-being and how these have been changing over time. To be able to do so, a coherent set of indicators on which information is available at regular intervals is required. Experience elsewhere demonstrates that such a range of indicators can provide a much more comprehensive picture of the complex and often varied ways in which child well-being is evolving. This suggests that initiation of a regular monitoring report on the well-being of Irish children may be the best way to focus attention on the data improvements needed to make that exercise even more valuable.

Chapter 8

Conclusions

8.1 AIM OF THE STUDY

Child income poverty had risen substantially in Ireland by the late 1980s, and a substantial gap had opened up at that point between poverty rates for children and for adults. The relative position of children versus adults also worsened in a number of other industrialised countries around that time, but the extent of child income poverty in Ireland appeared to be exceptionally high. The macro-economic environment in Ireland has been very different since then, with stagnation replaced by economic growth, with this growth reaching record levels since 1994. This study has used household survey data to explore in depth the evolution of child poverty in Ireland since the late 1980s, and to put child poverty in Ireland in a comparative perspective. It has identified the main factors producing poverty for Irish children and how these have been changing over time. It has also brought out the importance of going beyond household income in monitoring child welfare, by employing and developing other indicators at the level of the household and the child him or herself. The study is intended *inter alia* to contribute to the on-going development of the National Anti Poverty Strategy in this crucial area.

8.2 TRENDS IN RELATIVE INCOME POVERTY

Overall relative income poverty rates were first examined, and showed that the proportion of households falling below relative income poverty lines, and the proportion of persons in such households, rose both between 1987 and 1994 and between 1994 and 1997. Unemployment was almost as important a factor underlying relative income poverty in 1994 as in 1987, but by 1997 had declined significantly. Social welfare support rates — though increasing substantially in real terms — lagged behind average incomes between 1994 and 1997, and this played a central role in the observed increase in relative income poverty rates. With average incomes increasing rapidly in real terms, the numbers falling below poverty lines held fixed in real terms declined dramatically, particularly between 1994 and 1997.

The gap between relative income poverty rates for children and adults was fairly stable between 1987 and 1994, as the rates for each group rose. From 1994 to 1997, however, the poverty rates for children declined with the 50 per cent and 60 per cent relative income poverty lines while those for adults increased, producing a significant narrowing in that gap. With the 40 per cent line, however, the poverty rate for children increased, and more rapidly than for adults, partly reflecting the fact that this line has caught up on the support for families provided by some social welfare programmes, having previously been below them.

8.3 A COMPARATIVE PERSPECTIVE ON CHILD INCOME POVERTY IN IRELAND

A range of figures on the extent of relative income poverty for children in industrialised countries was presented, to put the Irish situation in its comparative context. By the late 1980s, Ireland was seen to have a relatively high child poverty rate on this basis compared with other European Community members. More up-to-date figures for 1994 show that Ireland in fact√N/P had the highest rate of child poverty, measured in this way, of any of the member states. Only Portugal and the UK had a child poverty rate nearly as high, and in many of the member countries the rate is half Ireland's or below. However other industrialised countries such as Australia, Canada and particularly the USA also had high child poverty rates measured in this way. Applying a common income poverty line across EU or industrialised countries gave a rather different picture, but Ireland in the mid-1990s would still have a relatively high poverty rate on that basis. While data do not allow these international comparisons to be updated beyond the mid-1990s, income poverty rates for Irish children have certainly been falling since then as unemployment in particular declined. This seems likely to still leave Ireland as among the EU countries with high relative income poverty rates for children, though now lower than the UK and Portugal.

8.4 POVERTY AND NON-MONETARY DEPRIVATION INDICATORS

Non-monetary indicators were also employed, together with income, to characterise more comprehensively the evolution of child poverty. Like relative income poverty lines, measures combining those lines with experience of basic deprivation showed children at a substantial disadvantage vis-à-vis adults in 1987 and 1994. Unlike those relative lines, however, these combined income and deprivation measures showed no narrowing in that gap between 1994 and 1997, with deprivation levels for adults declining more rapidly than children on average. As a result, in 1997 about 17 per cent of children were in households both below 60 per cent of mean equivalised income and experiencing basic deprivation, compared with about 9 per cent of adults. Compared with children below the relative income lines alone, a smaller proportion of the children meeting the combined income and deprivation poverty criteria were in households headed by a self-employed person or farmer and more are in households where the head is unemployed.

8.5 CHILD INCOME POVERTY DYNAMICS

Since cross-section income measures alone do not tell us all we need to know about which children are in poverty, sustained low income, as indicated by analysis of longitudinal data on income dynamics, is more likely to be a good indicator of need. Using the first two waves of the European Community Household Survey data for Ireland, income poverty persistence was examined in order to illustrate the value of dynamic analysis. The results showed, for example, income mobility was common for those on very low incomes — below 40 per cent of the median. By contrast, of those between 40 per cent and 50 per cent of the median in Wave 1, only 17 per cent had risen to above 60 per cent by Wave 2. Even at this early stage, such findings show how information on both income dynamics and non-monetary indicators of household welfare and deprivation levels can substantially complement one another in helping policy-makers to identify and target poor children. As more panel data becomes available, it will be possible using longitudinal data to directly link income and deprivation dynamics.

8.6 MEASURING CHILD WELL-BEING

The non-monetary indicators in the household surveys analysed here tell us about the living standards of households containing children: they do not serve as direct measures of living standards or deprivation for the children themselves. The situation where children are in poverty because of insufficient sharing of resources within the household will not be captured, either with conventional income measures or with the deprivation indicators we have available. A limited set of individual-level indicators has been developed for inclusion in the 1999 wave of the Living in Ireland survey, including some relating to children, and these will be analysed in a separate project for the Combat Poverty Agency.

More broadly, measures of poverty and deprivation can be seen as key indicators of the more wide-ranging concept of child well-being. It would be enormously valuable to be able to place poverty and deprivation levels in their broader setting, by also presenting a battery of other indicators relating to other aspects of children's well-being and how these have been changing over time. A review of the literature on children's well-being has recently been completed for the Combat Poverty Agency by Costello (1999). Perhaps the most notable recent innovation in this context has been the development of a limited but broad set of official indicators of child well-being in the USA, on which an annual monitoring report produced by the Federal Government is now based. Another recent study of child welfare in the member states of the European Union emphasises the limitations of the available indicators, and the need both to analyse existing data from a children's perspective and to develop new regular sources of statistics at European level. This applies with equal force in the Irish context. An intensive review of existing sources followed by initiation of a regular monitoring report on the well-being of Irish children may be the best way to focus attention on data improvements needed to make that exercise even more valuable.

8.7 RECENT DEVELOPMENTS AND CURRENT POLICY CONTEXT

The household survey data on which this study has drawn goes up to 1997. Very rapid economic growth has been sustained since then, bringing with it further pronounced falls in unemployment and in long-term unemployment, and with social welfare support rates increasing in real terms but lagging behind other incomes. This represents very much a continuation of the underlying trends seen over the 1994–97 period, and is likely to have had a broadly similar impact on child poverty. It seems likely that the gap between relative income poverty rates for children versus adults has continued to narrow, and that deprivation levels have continued to fall.

Since the comparative data currently available relates to the mid-1990s when unemployment here was even higher than in 1997, Ireland's ranking among EU countries in terms of relative income poverty for children should have improved significantly. However, more up-to-date figures would probably still show Ireland as among a group including Portugal and the UK with higher relative income poverty rates for children than other EU members. A comparison of Ireland and the UK with other industrialised countries brings out that unemployment does not convey the whole story as far as access by families to income from work is concerned. Ireland and the UK have particularly high percentages of households with children with no one in employment. This reflects both the extent of inactivity among working-age adults (which encompasses not only unemployment but illness and disability, education and working full-time in the home) and the way in which worklessness is concentrated in particular households.

Ireland and the UK also have similar structures for providing income support for families with children through the benefit and tax systems, with Ireland having a particularly low level of support compared with other EU countries,[1] and it is worth bringing out key issues for policy in this crucial area. The State has a variety of objectives in assisting families with the costs of child-rearing, which include not only avoiding or alleviating child poverty, but also helping redistribute resources across

---

[1] See Bradshaw, J., Ditch, J, Holmes, H. and Whiteford, P. (1993) *Support for Children: A Comparison of Arrangements in Fifteen Countries.* London: HMSO.

the life-cycle, sharing the costs of children across the community, and promoting efficiency in the labour market. A number of different instruments are also employed. Child Benefit provides an untaxed monthly amount for each dependent child, with (currently) a higher amount paid for third and subsequent children. Additional payments for each child dependant are made to those receiving support from the various regular weekly social welfare transfer schemes. Family Income Supplement also provides cash transfers to those in work on low incomes and with dependent children, with the amount varying with the level of (after-tax) earnings and the number of children. There has been no general tax relief to families with children since child tax allowances were abolished in 1986. There are, however, child additions to the tax exemption limits which determine the level at which one enters the tax net. The tax treatment of married couples versus single individuals could also be seen as an indirect way of assisting families with children, though this interpretation was among the issues contested in recent highly-charged debates about moving towards a greater degree of individualisation of income tax.

These instruments have different distributional and incentive effects, as has been brought out in, for example, Callan, O'Donoghue and O'Neill (1995). The best mix of instruments and the balance between them depends on the balance between what may be to some extent competing objectives — promoting horizontal equity, reducing child poverty, reducing disincentives, and ensuring that resources go to improving the lot of the children themselves. As discussed in detail in previous studies, targeting through the income tax system is regressive (though less so now that a tax credit system is in operation), failing to benefit those with incomes too low to be in the tax net. Child dependent additions to regular weekly social welfare payments do reach many of those on low incomes, but can contribute to serious unemployment traps. Trying to offset these effects through targeted payments to those in work on low pay runs the risk of pushing these disincentive effects a little further up the income distribution, exacerbating poverty traps. Child tax exemptions assist only those on the margins of the tax net, and can seriously worsen poverty traps.

Universal Child Benefit assists all those with children in meeting the costs involved, assists those on low incomes more than others relative to their incomes, and does not distort parental choices about for example labour force participation. It also directly helps mothers of dependent children, whether working outside the home or not, since the payment is generally made to the mother. It is not particularly well targeted in terms of concentrating resources on the poor, though, and a substantial increase is costly precisely because it is universal. For that reason my colleague Tim Callan and I have argued for some years for a strategy which substantially increases Child Benefit, but covers some of the cost by making it subject to income tax and clawing back some of the increase by reducing additional payments for child dependants (see, for example, Nolan, 1993; Callan, O'Neill and O'Donoghue, 1995).

In recent budgets Child Benefit has been the primary route through which extra resources for child support have been channelled, with child additional payments for social welfare recipients being effectively frozen since 1994, but no change in the tax status of Child Benefit has been implemented. The increases in Child Benefit have been quite substantial, representing approximately a doubling in the value of the payment in real terms since 1994. For those relying on social welfare, however, the freezing of the child dependant additions in nominal terms has meant that the overall value of their child income support has increased by only about 15-20 per cent in real terms over that period.

To see the extent to which Child Benefit does in fact go to those below relative income poverty lines, we can look first at the distribution of this transfer among households in the 1997 Living in Ireland survey. Table 8.1 shows that the precise figure depends on the equivalence scale employed to adjust income for the differing needs of households of different size and composition, but broadly speaking about 40 per cent of total Child Benefit then went to households falling below the 60 per cent relative income line.

Table 8.1: Percentage of Child Benefit Going to Households Below Relative Income Thresholds, Alternative Equivalence Scales, 1997

Relative Income Line	% Going to Households below Line		
	1/0.66/0.33	*1/0.6/0.4*	*1/0.7/0.5*
40 per cent line	14.8	17.7	19.9
50 per cent line	27.0	29.2	32.3
60 per cent line	39.4	41.1	43.6

Looking at the whole income distribution, Table 8.2 shows that less than half of total Child Benefit went to the top half of the household income distribution in the 1997 sample. Only about 10 per cent of the total went to the top 20 per cent of households in terms of equivalised income.

In order to bring this up to date and bring out the impact of a specific policy option, we can use the ESRI's SWITCH tax/benefit simulation model to look at the impact of a substantial increase in Child Benefit. The database for this model can be updated or projected into the future to reflect changes in incomes from different sources, the level of employment and unemployment, and demographic changes, and here we use such a projection for 2002. We take as base the policy for the year 2000 put in place in the recent Budget. That policy is then indexed in line with forecast earnings growth to the year 2002. We then consider the impact of an increase in Child Benefit of

£21.70 per month or about £5 per week, costing in total approximately £250 million per annum.

Table 8.2: Percentage of Child Benefit Going to Households by Equivalised Disposable Income Decile, Alternative Equivalence Scales, 1997

	% of Child Benefit Going to Households in Decile		
	1/0.66/0.33	*1/0.6/0.4*	*1/0.7/0.5*
Bottom	18.4	19.5	21.2
2	7.8	7.4	11.1
3	8.0	7.4	7.3
4	9.6	10.6	7.2
5	10.9	11.2	12.0
6	13.5	12.9	12.2
7	10.6	11.7	10.9
8	10.0	8.7	8.8
9	6.5	6.3	6.1
Top	4.7	4.1	3.1

Now, looking at the narrower tax unit or nuclear family rather than the household, we see from Table 8.3 that this additional expenditure would give the largest percentage increase in disposable income to those at the very bottom of the income distribution. Each of the bottom six deciles sees an increase of more than 1 percentage point in income, whereas those in the top two deciles see an increase of less than half a percentage point.

Table 8.3: Average Gain from Simulated Increase in Child Benefit by Tax Unit (Equivalised) Disposable Income Decile

Decile	% Gain from Increase in Child Benefit
Bottom	4.7
2nd	1.5
3rd	1.1
4th	1.2
5th	1.6
6th	1.2
7th	0.8
8th	0.6
9th	0.4
Top	0.3

This pattern of average gains in percentage terms must be seen against the background of rising income levels by decile. When we look at the distribution of the extra spending, Table 8.4 shows that the bottom decile does in fact receive more than 10 per cent of this spending, but the second and third deciles from the bottom receive considerably less. By contrast the top decile, despite its relatively low average increase in percentage terms, still receives one-tenth of the extra spending. Overall, the bottom half of the distribution receives just under half the additional spending on Child Benefit. This is less concentrated in the bottom half of the distribution than the pattern shown in Table 8.2 primarily because it refers to the narrower family unit rather than to the broader household. Nonetheless, it is still in marked contrast with support provided through relief on income tax, little of which would go towards the bottom two or three deciles.

Table 8.4: Distribution Across Tax Units by (Equivalised) Dispos-able Income Decile of the Gains from a Simulated Increase in Child Benefit

Decile	% of the Gains from Increase in Child Benefit
Bottom	11.3
2nd	6.5
3rd	5.6
4th	8.3
5th	16.2
6th	14.1
7th	11.0
8th	9.6
9th	7.5
Top	10.0

As the UK Chancellor of the Exchequer put it succinctly in his 1998 Budget, "child benefit remains the fairest, the most effi-cient and the most cost-effective way of recognising the extra costs and responsibilities borne by all parents". He also noted at the time, however, that were child benefit to be further in-creased, there would be a case for introducing tax, at least at the higher rate, on these payments. The case for substantially increasing and taxing child benefit has equal force in the Irish case. The fact that Child Benefit is normally paid to the mother and that the income tax system is being moved towards greater individualisation does not weaken this case. In the UK, indeed, income tax is already assessed mostly on an individual basis, and assessments of the policy options there (notably Clark and McCrae 1998) make clear that this does not mean that child benefit could only be taxed as the individual income of the per-son receiving it. It remains possible within a mostly individual-ised income tax system to treat child benefit as joint income of the couple, so that it could for example be taken as the income of the partner with the highest marginal tax rate and taxed at that rate.

Apart from child income support generally, the best way of assisting families with the costs of child-care has been the focus of particularly heated debate in recent years. A range of options was discussed in for example the report of the Commission on the Family (1998), without reaching agreement on the best way forward, and this issue is now being addressed by a working group under the new Partnership for Prosperity and Fairness. Without going into the complexities involved, a focus on child poverty brings out the importance of developing childcare support mechanisms which serve to assist all those with children, rather than only those in the tax net. Preferably, this should also be done without distorting parental choices about caring for children in or outside the home. Both these considerations point towards the advantages of universal payments rather than tax relief.

A range of concrete proposals aimed at tackling child poverty in Ireland has recently been put forward by the *Open Your Eyes to Child Poverty Initiative,* a joint initiative of the Combat Poverty Agency, the Children's Rights Alliance, Barnardos, the National Youth Council and the Society of St. Vincent de Paul. These proposals cover not only income adequacy but also education, and the needs of specific groups such as Traveller children and young people, children and young people with disabilities, and those out of home. This is particularly timely given the government's recent decision to prepare a National Children's Strategy. At the time of writing this is at the consultation stage, but the intention to set up an Office of Ombudsman for Children, which will have a role in promoting the welfare of children, has already been announced.

The new National Agreement, the Programme for Prosperity and Fairness, also includes some significant commitments in the area of child poverty. There is a commitment to increase substantially Child Benefit over the period of the Programme, with a priority focus towards £100 per month for the third and subsequent children. Child dependent additions will be payable to all social welfare recipients where the child is under 22 and in full-time education. There are also specific commitments directed at early childhood education and literacy, early school-leaving, back-to-school costs, the special educational needs of Travellers and of children and young people with disabilities, and at homelessness. In addition, broader measures aimed at improving the adequacy of social welfare support levels, targeting tax reductions to the lower paid, and other measures included as part of a £1.5 billion Social Inclusion package could have a significant impact on child poverty and well-being.

The National Anti Poverty Strategy will play a key role in marshalling these resources and monitoring progress in reducing poverty. The case for a specific NAPS target focusing on child poverty is currently being considered by the government, and such a target would indeed be a valuable way of making commitment concrete and concentrating effort. The benign economic environment projected for the next decade offers a unique opportunity to seriously tackle child poverty in Ireland, and the success of some of our European partners shows what can be achieved.

References

Barry, F. ed. (1999). *Understanding Ireland's Economic Growth*, London: Macmillan.

Bradbury, B. and M. Jantti (1999). *Child Poverty Across Industrialized Nations*, Innocenti Occasional Papers, Economic and Social Policy Series 71, Florence: UNICEF.

Bradley, J., FitzGerald, J., Honohan, P. and Kearney, I. (1997). "Interpreting the Recent Irish Growth Experience", in Duffy, D., FitzGerald, J., Kearney, I. and Shortall, F. eds., *Medium-Term Review: 1997-2003*, Dublin: The Economic and Social Research Institute.

Callan, T., Layte, R., Nolan, B., Watson, D., Whelan, C. T., Williams, J., & Maître, B. (1999), *Monitoring Poverty Trends: Data from the 1997 Living in Ireland Survey*, Dublin: Stationery Office/Combat Poverty Agency.

Callan, T., Nolan, B. and Whelan, C.T. (1993) "Resources, Deprivation and the Measurement of Poverty", *Journal of Social Policy*, 22 (2), 141-172.

Callan, T., Nolan, B., Whelan, B.J. Hannan, D.F. with Creighton, S. (1989) *Poverty, Income and Welfare in Ireland*, General Research Series No. 146, Dublin: The Economic and Social Research Institute.

Callan, T., Nolan, B., Whelan, B.J., Whelan, C.T. and Williams, J. (1996). *Poverty in the 1990s: Evidence from the Living in Ireland Survey*, General Research Series Paper 170, Dublin: Oak Tree Press.

Callan, T., O'Neill, C. and O'Donoghue, C. (1995). *Supplementing Family Income*, Policy Research Series Paper 23, Dublin: Economic and Social Research Institute.

Cantillon, S. and Nolan, B. (1998). "Are Married Women More Deprived than their Husbands?", *Journal of Social Policy*, 27, 2, 151-171.

Cantillon, S. and Nolan, B. (2000). "Can Gender Differences in Poverty Within Households Be Measured Using Non-Monetary Indicators?", *Feminist Economics*, forthcoming.

Central Statistics Office (1984). *Household Budget Survey 1980: Detailed Results*, Dublin : Stationery Office.

Clark, T. and McCrae, J. (1998). *Taxing Child Benefit*, Commentary 74, London: Institute for Fiscal Studies.

Commission on the Family (1998). *Strengthening Families for Life, Final Report*, Dublin: Stationery Office.

Costello, L. (1999). *A Literature Review of Children's Well-Being*, Report for the Combat Poverty Agency, mimeo.

Eurostat (1999). *First Results from the European Community Household Panel Survey*, Luxembourg: Publications Office of the European Community.

Federal Interagency forum on Child and Family Statistics (1999). *America's Children: Key National Indicators of Well-Being, 1999*, Washington D.C.: US GPO.

Hagenaars, A., de Vos, K. and Zaidi, M. A. (1994). *Poverty Statistics in the Late 1980s: Research Based on Micro-data,* Luxembourg: Office for Official Publications of the European Community.

Hallerod, B. (1995). "The Truly Poor: Direct and Indirect Measurement of Consensual Poverty in Sweden", *European Journal of Social Policy*, 5 (2), 111-29.

Hauser, R.M., Brown, B.V. and W.R. Prosser eds. (1997). *Indicators of Children's Well-Being*, New York: Russell Sage.

Howarth, C., Kenway, P., Palmer, G. and Street, C. (1998). *Monitoring Poverty and Social Exclusion: Labour's Inheritance*, York: Joseph Rowntree Foundation.

Institute of Social Studies Advisory Service (1990). *Poverty in Figures: Europe in the Early 1980s*, Luxembourg: Eurostat.

Jenkins, S.P. (1991) "Poverty measurement and the within-household distribution: agenda for action", *Journal of Social Policy*, 20 (Part 4), pp. 457-83.

Mack, J. and Lansley, S. (1985). *Poor Britain*, London: Allen and Unwin.

Mayer, S. (1993). "Living Conditions among the Poor in Four Rich Countries", *Journal of Population Economics*, 6, 261-286.

Mayer, S. and Jencks, C. (1988). "Poverty and the Distribution of Material Hardship", *Journal of Human Resources*, 24 (1), 88-114.

Micklewright, J. and Stewart, K. (1999). "Is Child Welfare Converging in the European Union?", Innocenti Occasional Papers, Economic and Social Policy Series 69, Florence: UNICEF.

Muffels, R. (1993) "Deprivation Standards and Style of Living Indices", in Berghman, J. and Cantillon, B. (1993) *The European Face of Social Security*, Aldershot: Avebury.

National Anti-Poverty Strategy (1997). *Sharing in Progress: National Anti-Poverty Strategy*, Dublin, Stationery Office.

National Anti-Poverty Strategy (1999). *Social Inclusion Strategy: 1998/99 Annual Report of the Inter-Departmental Policy Committee of the National Anti-Poverty Strategy*, Dublin, Stationery Office.

Nolan, B. (1993). *Reforming Child Income Support*, Dublin: Combat Poverty Agency.

Nolan, B. and Farrell, B. (1990). *Child Poverty in Ireland*, Dublin: Combat Poverty Agency.

Nolan, B. and Callan, T., (eds.), (1994). *Poverty and Policy in Ireland*, Dublin: Gill and Macmillan.

Nolan, B. and C. Whelan, (1996). *Resources, Deprivation and Poverty*, Oxford: Clarendon Press.

OECD (1998) Employment Outlook, Paris: OECD.

Rottman, D.B. (1994). *Allocating Resources Within Irish Families*, Dublin: Combat Poverty Agency.

Townsend, P. (1979). *Poverty in the United Kingdom*, Harmondsworth: Penguin.